A Heart of Gold:

LESSONS ON THE PATH OF LOVING KINDNESS

DEDICATION

This book is dedicated
to those who walk the path of Loving Kindness.

Author Photo: Dee Soderstrom
Cover Design: Sarabeth Jones

A Heart of Gold: Lessons on the Path of Loving Kindness

INTRODUCTION — 5

PART I: FOUNDATIONS OF LOVING KINDNESS — 10

Why Loving Kindness? — 11

What is Loving Kindness? — 18

Laying a Foundation of Compassion — 26

Know Thyself to Love Thyself — 33

All We Need is Love — 44

Love for the World — 52

PART II: STORIES FROM MY LOVING KINDNESS PATH — 58

A Child's Heart Full of Love — 59

Broken Hearts Grow Beautiful New Things — 66

Coming Home to Mama Italy — 73

My Journey into Yoga, Shamanism and Loving Kindness — 89

New York Sangha — 106

4

PART III: THE PRACTICES OF LOVING KINDNESS

114

Practicing Loving Kindness   115

Creating Expansive Space   118

Meditation   122

Silence   126

Creativity   129

Listening   132

Writing   135

Gratitude   138

Retreats   141

Slowness   147

MY LOVING KINDNESS BLESSING

152

APPENDIX I:
SACRED PRACTICES
FOR THE SEASONS

154

APPENDIX II:
DIY LOVING KINDNESS RETREAT

173

I've been experimenting with Loving Kindness for most of my adult life, long before I really knew what it was.

It all began with my desire to really know myself, deal with my suffering, and face my truth. I wanted to figure out how to live with genuine compassion for myself and others.

My central life questions have always been about how I can be a more loving person, accept what I have no control over, and find a way to live that feels genuine.

Loving Kindness has been how I both increase my own happiness and bring happiness to others.

That may sound overly simple or even like I am suggesting a path that is without suffering or pain, but Loving Kindness does not mean life is without difficulty. However, when I am close to Loving

Kindness, I navigate life's hard places in a way that feels safe, loving and connected. This is something I've yearned for ever since I was a child. Even then, I possessed a strong knowing of how disconnected we are as a culture.

Loving Kindness was with me as a child, but I also learned it through suffering.

The true fruit of Loving Kindness has grown in my life in two unexpected places: in yoga and in Italy.

Yoga found me one day at the public library. As a young mother, one of my weekly rituals was spending time at the library where my children attended reading hour. I would explore the shelves with my time alone and take home books that opened up a dreamy life.

One day at the library, a small book on yoga literally fell off the shelf as I was pulling another book from the travel section about Italy. These two books were all of a sudden side by side in my hands. Quite auspicious even then.

Both books came home with me. It's my earliest memory of falling in love with yoga and Italy. I stayed up reading until 3 am. Those books and the wisdom I learned were the first inklings of Loving Kindness.

It would be several more years before I visited Italy and even longer before I discovered the ancient rhythms there that taught me more Loving Kindness, but yoga quickly became a safe haven for me, a place where I could know my body.

Yoga seemed almost magical. Everything about it said yes.

I was pursuing a degree in health and wellness and was hungry for new books, theories, and teachings. I started practicing at home by looking at small photos from the book, Richard Hittleman's 28-day yoga program. The writing was clear and simple.

Soon I became completely mesmerized with yoga in my own little universe. It was the first time in my life where I felt that I didn't have to go hard or achieve in my body.

Most of the people in my circle only knew of yoga through esoteric images or strange stories and practices, so in these early days of yoga, I practiced solo. Perhaps it was the lack of the social aspect that made it so that yoga would become for me a way to reliably fill my well.

I was involved with classical ballet for ten years from the age of six. It was a punishing world of body shame where there were endless practices, recitals, routines and a very cold teacher from Russia, Mrs. Woody, may she rest in peace. She would walk behind us at the bar and tap our heads with a wooden stick to get us in line (with a cigarette dangling from the corner of her mouth).

I both loved and hated those ballet years. I loved the embodied movement, my fellow dancers, the beauty of putting together a piece and performing it at the recital. But the art of ballet is about developing perfectionism. Remaining bird thin, practicing relentlessly, constantly dieting and the competitive culture took away all the joy of ballet for me.

So when I found yoga, I rediscovered the embodied movement I had loved in ballet. For the next decade I practiced on my own at home. There really were not many classes or teachers around where I lived. This was the 1980s and yoga had not burst onto the marketplace.

My practice was solitary and developed in the spirit of going inward. Yoga is how I healed my ballet body trauma.

Practicing yoga steadily for a number of years has transformative qualities. For me it brought the healing of my scars and wounds. It brought Loving Kindness.

I've been on a spiritual healing path from a very young age. Naturally drawn to it, mostly on my own. It's who I am and what I do each and every day.

I've learned that I can begin to trust myself through the practice of compassion and Loving Kindness.

The path of Loving Kindness has a quality of hope.

It feels like a dear friend that takes our hand and assures us that things will work out one way or the other, even though we have a long way to go.

Part One:

FOUNDATIONS
OF LOVING KINDNESS

Why Loving Kindness?

Love and Compassion are necessities, not luxuries.
Without them, humanity cannot survive.
Dalai Lama

Nothing in my entire life has made more sense to me than the beautiful teachings on Loving Kindness, compassion and self-love. It's how I aspire to live and be on this earth. Conversely nothing has been more challenging than my deep desire to embrace Loving Kindness wholeheartedly, and let it be my safe protective container for life.

Loving Kindness is the spiritual quality where I believe all the secrets to happiness and joy await.

At its core, Loving Kindness makes the world a more tolerant and forgiving place. This idea is not idealistic or pie in the sky. It is opening to truth without bypassing reality.

At the heart of Loving Kindness is deep care and consideration for humankind. We may consider it a road map to finding peace and calm in a world that always tests our will. This is true for all humans. None of us are immune to pain, sadness, heartache and impermanence. Loving Kindness may be the antidote we're seeking.

There will never be an end to suffering and there will never be an end to personal pain, growth and evolution, but Loving Kindness offers us a practice where we can sit down in our bodies and feel our way into our hearts. Its essence will always be amongst the top treasured, tried and true practices for grounding and centering. Loving Kindness will always lead to finding peace and more happiness.

Loving Kindness is medicine to keep us going. To realize life is worth it. To keep finding beauty, to know how to appreciate beauty and see it in all sentient beings. This is the dream of life. When anger, sadness, confusion, frustration and doubt consume us, if we learn to return to the practice of Loving Kindness, it will take our hand and lead us back home.

Anyone in the world, anywhere, no matter what age, gender, background, race or socioeconomic structure can learn how to weave Loving Kindness into ordinary life. Loving Kindness is universal in its accessibility.

All we need is a desire to begin.

And time. Dear heart, you need time.

This book is part memoir, part guide, and part storytelling as I weave the pages of this Loving Kindness journey into tales of my own life story and travels, but from the outset I want it to be a book filled with lessons that are deeply practical for also weaving Loving Kindness into your own life. I want you to find within yourself your own heart of gold.

So at the end of each chapter you will find a simple practice that you can use to grow Loving Kindness in your life, so that as you read, you can experience the deep joys and benefits of this spiritual quality. You can use this book over any number of months or weeks to give yourself time to develop the qualities discussed and the practices provided. And you can return to them again and again in the years to come.

So right here in the introduction, before we go any further, I want to give you the opportunity to set an intention towards Loving Kindness. Towards giving yourself the time you need to deepen the practice of loving yourself and others.

Intention Setting

MEDITATION PRACTICE

Find a quiet place to sit. You can use a chair or your yoga mat or a meditation cushion.

Read the meditation below a few times and then close your eyes for 5-10 minutes while you set an intention for the development of Loving Kindness in your life. Afterwards spend about five more minutes answering the journal questions below.

Meditation:

Sankalpa is the Sanskrit word for intention. Say it out loud a few times. Set a *Sankalpa* to give yourself the time you need to develop Loving Kindness. Quietly consider where you can give yourself some space for this task. Is it in the morning? Is there an hour in the middle of your day that you could use?

CHOOSE A PHRASE
FOR YOUR INTENTION
THAT YOU REPEAT A FEW TIMES.

A few examples:

I devote myself to Loving Kindness.

Loving Kindness, be my guide.

I am bringing Loving Kindness
to my life.

Each time you sit to meditate or step onto your mat, come back to this phrase and repeat it to yourself. It is always there for you as your loving guide.

Your thoughts and intentions give your life enormous power. For today, we want to ease into the practice of Loving Kindness. You have plenty of time. There is enough space. Be kind to yourself as you think about where you want to see Loving Kindness come to your life.

Journaling Questions

How would you define Loving Kindness?

Journaling Questions

Write down any thoughts you want to remember about setting your intention.

What is Loving Kindness?

Carry out a random act of kindness,
with no expectation of reward, safe in the knowledge
that one day someone might do the same for you.
Princess Diana

Maitri is the Sanskrit word for Loving Kindness and it embodies friendship and generosity and acts of love.

We direct this *Maitri* towards ourselves, viewing ourselves with compassion and love.

Maitri toward ourselves does not look like a self-improvement plan.

We are not trying to throw our current selves away in order to replace them with something better.

When we walk on this path towards Loving Kindness, we are not guaranteeing that life will not be difficult. We cannot be certain that things will always go smoothly or that we will never hurt or feel angry anymore.

Instead, we listen carefully to our hearts.

Loving Kindness means we attempt to make good friends with who we are, right here and now.

Loving Kindness is not a hard push for change.

Hardening into change or forcing never feels right.

You know this pattern. You have probably experienced it. You start something new, go really hard at it and then at some point, you crash and burn. It wasn't sustainable because it was too aggressive or because it had no heart.

It wasn't in the spirit of self-love or kindness.

Loving Kindness is a way into our heart that isn't aggressive, pushy or demanding.

It wants us to really know who we are, right now in our current state of mind. Not in some future idealized time. This is the brilliance that we all share. We begin at the beginning, not at an idealized place far off and dreamy. It's right here, right now, just as we are. All of our messy, hurt, and confused selves. We do not have to have everything together to begin.

Loving Kindness is choosing to be with ourselves and to witness where we are, in this time and place. To be in whatever place we find ourselves with compassion and grace.

This is what makes Loving Kindness a fresh approach. We accept who we are in our current state instead of subscribing to outside messages that we must change. This acceptance will ground our practice, which becomes free of pressure and self-loathing.

Maitri means we still have issues. We all have daily frustrations.

Wherever we are on our spiritual journey, life gets in the way. All kinds of influences can take us off course. Sometimes our own moods or lack of energy can derail us.

When this happens, we can allow curiosity to emerge about any subtle aggression against who we really are.

We can raise our consciousness about the ways in which we are trying to do everything "the right way" so that we can be ahead of the game or so that all will go "according to plan?"

These are the areas in which we need Loving Kindness to extend fully into our lives. When we give ourselves permission to receive love even when frustrations with our practice arise, we experience a softening.

It is when we soften that a shift will most likely occur in our practice.

In Buddhist teachings, Loving Kindness is defined as friendliness, compassion, joy and equanimity. It's how we remember how much love, beauty and goodness there is in the world. We need help remembering. In fact we need more help remembering than we do learning new things. Time to unfetter and untether the knots in our mind. To let fresh air blow through our thoughts and cleanse them.

Loving Kindness in practice requires us to place our attention on our intentions. It's a way of living where we are learning how to truly be present, to open our hearts to what is happening within us, and around us.

In the Buddhist tradition, we are all said to possess basic goodness. This way of thinking gives us a beautiful way to tend our whole self. It encourages us not to separate, divide and conquer.

Loving Kindness is how we relate to our basic goodness. It's a safe haven. It will nurture our heart, heal our soul. It's how we see beauty.

We need ways of noticing all the beautiful things that happen in life, just because. This can include the wonders of sunrise, sunset, sky and stars. Stories about how humans touch each others' hearts through their presence. The human spirit and its big capacity.

How we heal, how we grow, how we stay together.

At the heart of the practice is self-love and compassion. These are the roots of Loving Kindness. It begins inside of us and grows outward. It's a way to understand our life and give it a deeper meaning. It reminds us not to polarize, to split, to side against or to narrow our view.

Loving Kindness is even a way to make peace with our enemies, including the parts of ourselves that feel unlovable.

We all have the ability to wake up and know ourselves.

In meditation, think of Loving Kindness as the light on the path.

As we explore and expand, we are moving toward the light, staying in the light, returning to the light. Soon we will begin to know how to return to the light when we experience hard times or dark days.

Meditation:

Allow yourself time today to practice slowing down and reflecting on one way you can be kinder to yourself, here and now. Enter your quiet space, return to your intention.

Reflect on the idea of Loving Kindness as light on the path. On what parts of your life do you need or desire this light of Loving Kindness to shine? Visualize the light sweeping in and around the areas that come to mind.

Journaling Questions

Spend some time writing about what is coming up for you. You can write about how your body feels and your general mood. You can journal desires and hopes or write about where you want to allow more Loving Kindness in your life.

Journaling Questions

Laying a Foundation of Compassion

Compassion is an action word with no boundaries.
Prince

Loving Kindness has three pillars. They are like the three legs of a stool. They build on each other, and the stool cannot remain upright if any one of them is missing.

These three pillars of Loving Kindness are:

Love for Self
Love for Others
Love for the World

I would argue that you have to begin and progress in that order, because it is impossible to truly love others when we do not love ourselves.

Our world doesn't have a great track record for teaching its citizens how to love themselves.

I already hear my young nieces talk about how they feel fat or ugly and it breaks my heart. I talk to them about self-love and they listen, hungry for more, but like all of us, they need lots of support. We need the messages of self-love to be continually around us every day until we are as saturated with them as we are with messages of self-loathing.

The first step on the journey of loving ourselves is to cultivate compassion.

I'm not talking about loving puppies and children and wanting the world to be a much more sane and loving place.

Of course we need to find ways to grow our compassion for the world, and all of the beings in it. We need to stay alert, fight for social justice and be very mindful about our actions, words and deeds.

But we cannot offer compassion to anyone else that we have not first given to ourselves.

At the base of an outward compassion practice is a call to begin practicing compassion with ourselves. We start by noticing how compassion begins within our own heart and mind, and grows outward.

How we apply deep compassion for our own process, pain, suffering and life will mean the world to others. We can know through our own internal deep experience what it means to walk in another's shoes. To witness the human experience from the inside out.

What I know to be true is that when I practice having compassion for myself, feeling tenderness for my own process and letting my heart rest into gentle abiding, I can see into another's experience and there is a great heart awakening.

Compassion is what happens before self love. Perhaps think of compassion as the seat of the three-legged stool. It provides the place to sit.

Adversity is the birthplace of our rising compassion. And the beginning of real personal growth. Without adversity we won't grow, because nothing is happening. The juice is in the parts of our lives where there is suffering, disappointment and sadness. We resist these basic truths so intensely, then we suffer even more. Even though most people intellectually get that life won't be without suffering or pain, we still behave as though we can avoid it, skip it or see it from afar.

This is why we suffer so deeply when painful things happen to us. We don't accept that they are coming, so we don't train for the arrival of pain. Then when it inevitably comes, we don't know what to do with it.

Compassion is how we begin to untether all the tangled parts. It's a safe haven and where we find love for our self, so that we can truly love another.

When we touch the face of love within, it's a path toward making peace with all our messy unlovable parts. Compassion is how we train for self-love and love of all the messy ugly parts of ourselves and life.

In order to understand why we should practice or how, we have to slow down and take time to feel, see and know who we really are.

Self-Compassion is how we love ourselves through everything we experience. It's how we relate to our basic goodness, and that of our fellow human beings.

Compassion teaches us how to not harm ourselves or others. No matter what. It's permission to soften and stop trying to fix everything.

Sweet relief. Gentle ease.

Once we understand how to touch our basic goodness, to feel what another can feel in their heart, we're close, so close.

Compassion is embracing that we are enough, right here and now.

Nothing else is needed.

Meditation
FOR GIVING
YOURSELF COMPASSION:

Take some time to quiet your heart as you begin your Loving Kindness practice today.

Let compassion begin simply.

Ask yourself these questions:

Where am I being harsh with myself? How can I get off my own back?

Can you bring compassion to those places where you expect more of yourself than of anyone else?

Journaling Questions

Is there one unloving behavior or phrase that you could release?

What would that look like?

Journaling Questions

Know Thyself to Love Thyself

*For all of us, love can be the natural state
of our own being; naturally at peace, naturally connected,
because this becomes the reflection of who we simply are.
Meditation teacher Sharon Salzberg on Loving Kindness*

Understanding how Loving Kindness helps us make peace with life happens one step at a time. The first step into peace is through self-love. Loving one's self is where you return home again and again as you learn to practice Loving Kindness.

Self-love means that we care for our own well being with an intentional and loving heart. We learn to love all the messy and imperfect parts, which all of us on the planet experience. We recognize that we're always evolving, and so is the world around us. Loved ones, partners, people, politics and the state of the world are always changing and life itself is completely impermanent. This is the very nature of life, both daunting and liberating.

We read often about self-love. People we admire or respect talk about it. When someone else tells us that they are trying to practice loving themselves, we affirm them and believe they are right to take care of themselves. But for some reason, we can go for years and years without stopping to consider that we too need self-love.

Maybe it sounds like something we feel we should do or something we will get around to when we feel we've earned it. Like a vacation. In our western society, we have cultivated the idea that stopping to take care of yourself means sacrificing something else more important. We might even equate it with weakness. You only give yourself a break when you are so stressed out that you physically and mentally cannot function.

Why do we feel we need to burnout before we can offer ourselves love?

One strong possibility is that we do not understand the peace and joy that the practice of loving ourselves will bring to our lives.

We spend a lot of time chasing after the shiny things that we think might make us happy. But then when they don't work, we are caught in feelings of frustration and hopelessness. We churn up anxiety and negativity when the diet, the new relationship or the new life plan does not work out. We are caught when we realize that wherever we go, there we are. We return again and again to destructive thoughts like, "I'll never be enough, my life won't be different after all, I can't have the joy I really desire."

Somewhere inside of us we might believe that we should learn how to live with more self-love by taking better care of our bodies, minds and hearts, but daily practice requires us to fully understand why this brings us more happiness. And understanding begins with getting to know ourselves through a tender heart.

All the great sages, yogis and spiritual teachers teach us to know thyself first.

In Tibetan Buddhism, the mind is seen as being dependent on the energy or wind air within the body. This subtle energy is called the "windhorse," or lungta. The life force called windhorse is the unlimited energy of basic goodness, Buddha nature, inherent wakefulness.

Basic goodness can be a beautiful starting point. A way to let self-love grow. To tenderly hold space for our own fragility. To see the deeper truths we all share.

We all crave peace of mind. Right mind, right action. It always begins with developing a loving acceptance of oneself. Inevitably in life, we get lost or make a decision that gets us off course. But this is how we grow. It's hard to accept the simple truth that if everything always went exactly as we wanted, we wouldn't grow.

Adversity is how we strengthen our self-love. By caring for our own well being and knowing that in order to grow we must take risks.

Life itself is undeniably fragile. Suffering is inevitable. Everything changes, it's the nature of our existence. We can't control anything even though we keep trying. It's that "keep trying" part that gets us all hooked.

We all experience heartbreak and rejection. No human who is really living life can escape that. Mostly we are lost in the idea that something should change or be different in order for us to be truly happy. We long for something other than what is happening right here and now.

Instead of living in reality or in the moment, we are lost in thoughts of what could or should be. We are lost in effort. It's like an itch that endlessly needs scratching. It's that wiggly uncomfortable feeling that something is not quite right. We think that there is something wrong with us (or we think that something is wrong with everyone else).

To courageously look into our deepest, most tender places of hurt is how we open the window and begin to cope. We can start by just taking a little peek.

In yoga the word for self study is Svadhyaya. It's how we learn to live into our most authentic self. Svadhyaya is not your annual review of your productivity. It's a loving gaze at what needs to come forth from your soul. It's letting the elephant in the room of your heart gently step into the light. If we're viewing our life as a pilgrimage of the heart, then we don't need to hide our yearnings away.

Whenever we feel words or phrases like, "stop, no more, it's over, I'm done," we are hearing a call for our souls to be witnessed and tended to.

Self-love is the basis for all loving relationships, and loving ourselves starts with learning how to be ok with who we are. So when the soul steps forward and you allow yourself to be seen by your own mind without judgment, but only with compassion, you are beginning to experience the practice of Loving Kindness.

Loving Kindness helps us get off the train of continuously suffering and longing to be a different version of ourselves. When we get off that train, we can sit still and know that we are okay just as we are.

Of course this practice is not easy, because the world is constantly trying to bring us back to a different wavelength, one of struggle and striving.

Women in particular have a really hard time leaning into self-love. We are so conditioned to care for children, partners, family members and others that we often come last. Culturally there is a huge push on women to excel at everything for everyone else, and then maybe if there are a few minutes left at the end of the day, they can squeeze in five minutes of yoga.

Self-love is one of our greatest struggles. Most women I know are exceedingly hard on themselves. We're pretty sure that we have to accomplish a huge list of things before we can be worthy of our own love, let alone anyone else's. We don't really like who we are so we keep trying to solve something, which keeps us stuck in an exhausting daily grind.

Often in order to let ourselves off the hook, we need one-on-one intimate helpers, guides, wise woman mentors.

Helping women tend to their own self-love has become my life's work. I began teaching yoga out of compassion for myself, and the women around me who need permission to love themselves, and I started leading sacred retreats and holistic coaching out of a desire to help women clear space, make time and embrace the importance of loving themselves.

I have had retreat students tell me that being on retreat is the first time in their lives that they actually felt self-love and had the space to fully embody it in real time.

I long for women to love themselves in daily practice, not

just once or twice in a lifetime. So I started offering free holistic coaching on my website in order to help more women embrace Loving Kindness. Finding someone to help you love yourself can be essential to giving yourself permission, but if no one is available right now or you find yourself in a place where you are not sure you can reach out for help, read these words from me out loud to yourself. Or you can listen to me read them in the complimentary resources section of the shop page on my website (radiantjane.com). You can come back to this affirmation of Loving Kindness in your life again and again.

Dear heart,

After all the time you have spent tending to others, now is your time.

You are a magnanimous human being and you deserve all of the love and tenderness life has to offer.

I give you permission to take your foot off the pedal. Your body won't tolerate the pedal-to-the-floor stress forever.

Your life is too precious not to generate more qualities of equanimity.

You need cozy little nooks of inner okay-ness.

You need a place for a respite. Where can you rest, dear one?

Your life is not a race to the finish line.

You are beautiful just as you are. Your heart, your soul, whatever is emerging as you begin to know yourself, it belongs. Nothing needs changing.

Practicing Loving Kindness is not a life change plan. It is already within you. Sit and know that you have everything within you that you need.

You are worthy of all the love you can give yourself in this lifetime.

You can love yourself without conditions and without limits.

You can start right now. When you forget, you can start again.

Every moment that you take your gaze inward and love yourself is a moment that you are coming home to your true self, who you really are.

May you know peace in those moments, dear heart.

Namaste.

Through my darkest and lightest moments, I've been able to soften and tenderly deal with life's complexities within the heart of Loving Kindness. At the root of it is compassion. In the beginning of my practice I was inspired to keep going whenever I sensed a glimmer in the darkness. When I paid attention and let myself go there, I found that accepting my own limitations, pettiness or shame was a really good starting point.

Loving Kindness is medicine to keep us going. To realize life is worth it. To keep finding beauty, to know how to appreciate beauty and see it in all sentient beings. This is the dream of life. When anger, sadness, confusion, frustration or doubt consumes us, we learn to return to the practice of Loving Kindness.

Real change usually comes tenderly in the night like a kiss from the Moon. It might take much longer than we imagine, but that is okay. We have time to really know ourselves, to be with ourselves from the inside out.

Life presents as it does each day for us. I love the teachings on interdependence. It speaks to our need to not polarize just to find order in a chaotic world. We live in such fortunate times. We have this tremendous opportunity to evolve. Right here and right now is the best place to start.

Meditation

FOR LOVING YOURSELF:

Read (or listen to) the affirmation of Loving Kindness in your life again. This time pause after you read and meditate.

Breathe softly through your nose, observing your breath. There is only this breath coming in, there is only this breath going out. Give yourself 10-15 minutes of sitting in this present moment.

Journaling Questions

Where do you need permission to practice self-love? Is there someone you could ask to help you?

Journaling Questions

Explore what loving yourself could look like.

All We Need Is Love

If I go into the place in myself that is love,
and you go into the place in yourself that is love,
we are together in love.
Then you and I are truly in love, the state of being love.
Ram Dass

Most of us would affirm the truth that all we need is love, but somehow we cannot seem to take that affirmation into practice. We live like we need a lot more than just love. Maybe that's why the Beatles repeat this very phrase over forty times in this classic song. It feels like they are working hard to try to get it through our heads. Or into our hearts.

Love for others is the second pillar of Loving Kindness. But if we are beginners on the path of Loving Kindness, we can't rush too quickly into loving those around us. If we're going to help heal the world, we've got to heal our own precious self first.

For some this feels counterintuitive or selfish, but being hard on ourselves goes hand in hand with being hard on our loved ones.

It's not a friendly way to live.

We need reminders to lighten up in the name of self-love and compassion.

We have to break out of the mode of trying to fix, change or enlighten. These are the practices of striving. When we leave striving to improve ourselves and others behind, we are able to accept the moment as it is. We love ourselves and others as we are. We enjoy life and are present to whatever comes.

All human life contains darkness, light and all the colors in between.

We are all in it together. We don't need to separate.

Some of us have obviously endured much more pain and suffering than others and some people live with more privilege, but all humans desire happiness and love. This desire is what binds us as a species.

We can recognize that desire in others no matter what container they offer it to us in.

People come to us in all kinds of ways. They can be complaining or anxious. They can be angry or irritable. Overjoyed and loud. Whatever arrives, we can know that what is needed is Loving Kindness.

Loving Kindness is soft and strong at the same time. Loving others requires us to soften, to be vulnerable. To give without expecting anything in return. Being vulnerable and strong is powerful when we open to it.

This does not mean we will sit down in a zen state at any given moment. Loving Kindness does not mean that we open ourselves to abuse or even a vindictive spirit. Sometimes the most compassionate thing we can do for a person is to release them.

But we always have access to a place where we can focus our intentions again. We love ourselves, and from that place of peace and harmony, we can offer love to others.

There is a wise teaching that arises from the Tibetan word, *Shenpa* that can help us as we seek to practice loving others.

Shenpa is the urge, the hook, that triggers our habitual tendency to close down or act out. We get hooked in that moment of tightening when we reach for relief. In order to get unhooked, we begin by recognizing that moment of unease and learn to relax in that moment.

Practicing *Shenpa* has been an enormous blessing in my life. Understanding why it's a good idea to "not take the bait" is a soothing balm for the times we feel most triggered.

Here's how it works. Let's say you are having a tense moment with your partner or co-worker. At one moment their face is open and they are listening to you, but then something quickly changes. They are no longer open, and it feels uncomfortable. Pause and observe. What is it that you are seeing?

You thought you were doing your best and you had the best of intentions, but someone isn't liking what's happening. There is a negative reaction.

This is *Shenpa*. It is usually translated as "attachment," but a more descriptive translation might be "hooked." When *Shenpa* hooks us, we're likely to get stuck. We could call *Shenpa* "that sticky feeling."

It's an everyday experience. Even a pose in yoga can take you there. At the most subtle level, we feel a tightening, a tensing, a feeling of anxiousness. Then we feel a sense of withdrawing, not wanting to be where we are. That's the hooked quality. Again, it can also be "taking the bait."

That tight feeling has the power to hook us into blame, anger, jealousy and other emotions which lead to words and actions that end up poisoning both ourselves and the people at whom we direct them.

Loving Kindness means we don't want our actions to end up adding to the suffering of the world, as opposed to taking away from the suffering of the world.

Shenpa thrives on the underlying insecurity of living in a world that is always changing. We experience this insecurity as a background of slight unease or restlessness. We all want some kind of relief from that unease, so we turn to what we enjoy without moderation: food, alcohol, drugs, work or shopping. In moderation, we can appreciate these tastes and their presence in our lives. But when we empower a person or a taste with the idea that they will bring us comfort or that they will remove our unease, we get hooked.

When we release people (and things) from that power, when we acknowledge that they cannot fulfill us, we can unhook ourselves. We sit with the unease. We love ourselves in the midst of the discomfort. We are free. And it is really only from this freedom that we can love others.

Meditation

FOR PRACTICING SHENPA:

In practicing with *Shenpa*, first we try to recognize it. The best place to do this is during meditation. Sitting practice teaches us how to open and relax to whatever arises, without picking and choosing. We do this by not following after the thoughts and learning to come back to the present moment. We learn to stay with the uneasiness, the tightening, the itch.

We observe people and situations just as they are, and accept them with all of our heart.

We stop trying to escape feelings of uneasiness. Because when we escape, we never get to the root of practice. The root is experiencing the itch as well as the urge to scratch, and then not acting it out.

Be gentle as you observe. Be curious about what you see. Can you return again and again from your thoughts to the present moment and accept it as it is?

Journaling Questions

Journal about *Shenpa*. Write about three moments you've had in the past few days where you've experienced *Shenpa* or you observed someone in a *Shenpa* moment. Write how it made you feel to witness that in yourself or in another.

Journaling Questions

Love For The World

The wisdom of the heart can be found
in any circumstance, on any planet, round or square.
It arises not through knowledge or images of perfection,
or by comparison or judgment, but by seeing with the eyes
of wisdom and the heart of loving attention,
by touching with compassion all that exists in our world.
Jack Kornfield

Loving Kindness helps the suffering of our world. It really is that simple.

When we practice Loving Kindness, we take away from the suffering of the world rather than adding to it.

Loving Kindness is benevolent and tender. Once we've offered it to ourselves, we are able to give it freely to others. Then we begin to know the beauty of life. We see others as beautiful and we give ourselves to the things in the world that build love and compassion.

It's not something we need to perfect or arrive at. Not even close. We let it inspire us to get out of bed every morning and seize life. It's how we make sense of living in a world that contains so much uncertainty, sadness, tragedy and sorrow.

When we are overwhelmed by the suffering in the world, our

practice of Loving Kindness comes to our rescue. Loving Kindness is not ignoring the world or putting our heads in the sand. On the contrary, a strong practice of Loving Kindness will manifest itself in actions. But without the practice, we have no peace or harmony to bring to the world.

Loving Kindness has a huge heart with big aspirations. It wants us to come on in and sample the goodness. It's yearning for us to be curious about how we approach our inevitable impermanence. To question the way we live, judge, spend our days. Loving Kindness leads and guides us to what we are supposed to do and be in the world.

It will look different for everyone, so you can't take someone else's way of loving the world and expect it to be your own. Your love for the world will be uniquely yours, growing out of your own practice of Loving Kindness.

Here are a few ways I have seen others love the world from their practice of Loving Kindness.

Providing a place for loved ones to gather and pouring out love on those who come, whether it is family, friends, children or strangers.

Offering plates of cookies to neighbors. Making food for those who are sick.

Taking a class to learn something new.

Volunteering time to be present with others whether it is in nursing homes, schools, refugee settlements or prisons.

Starting a foundation for a cause.

Creating anything whether it's a painting, a sculpture, a knitted scarf or handmade soap. Creativity adds to the joy of the world.

Your outpouring of love for the world will be a retreat for your soul, even if it requires much of you. Whatever it may be and however it shifts and changes over time, it will come from a place of loving yourself and loving others. Taking time to know yourself will lead you to how you are wired up to love the world.

A Meditation

FOR LOVING THE WORLD WHEN YOU ARE WEARY OF THE NEWS:

When we engage with the world around us through the media, we put ourselves at the midst of a storm. Finding your own way of knowing what is happening in the world is important, but equally important is how you engage and process what you take in. I would like to offer a suggestion that we can take a rest from judging, analyzing or trying to fix.

The heart gets weary and heavy and needs rest.

I take an annual one month sabbatical from Facebook. In addition to being rejuvenating, it helps me feel into my own intelligence, voice and essence outside the noise.

We're all finding our way through these times, and I will always advocate for pausing, meditating and practicing Loving Kindness, which is to be compassionate with myself, my loved ones, the entire world. Loving Kindness inspires me to hope for a better world that isn't separating, violent and unloving.

When I pause and enter deep silence, I notice huge shifts in my level of tolerance, creativity and healing.

Holding silence is the opposite of what you may think. Silence is not lonely, frightening or separating. Instead it's enlightening, comforting and loving.

For this meditation, if possible, take twenty-four hours to silence all the news. If you have taken in something especially heartbreaking in recent days, pause as often as possible over the next full day. Then fill the silence you have created with your hands lifted in front of you like you are offering your peace to the world.

You may have your own words for offering your peace and harmony to the hurting world, or you can borrow this blessing from the Buddha:

May all beings be happy.
May all beings be healthy.
May all beings be peaceful.
May all beings live with ease.

Be sure to include yourself in the blessing.

Journaling Questions

Journal about where you can bring silence to your life in order to allow your unique love for the world to emerge.

Part Two:

STORIES FROM MY
LOVING KINDNESS PATH

A Child's Heart Full of Love

The monsters of our childhood do not fade away,
neither are they ever wholly monstrous.
But neither, in my experience, do we ever reach a plane of
detachment regarding our parents, however wise and old we
may become. To pretend otherwise is to cheat.
John le Carre

When I was very young my Dad always used to say, "Jane pay attention. Pay attention to the world we live in, the people around you and how you feel about things."

As a deeply sensitive child, it was easy for me to take his instruction to heart.

On November 23, 1963 I came home from kindergarten and my Dad was sitting on the sofa in front of the television crying. John F. Kennedy had been killed.

This is my earliest memory of noticing suffering and feeling empathy. I remember that in those moments, I felt so much love not just for him, but for all of the people who were suffering because of this national tragedy.

I was only five years old, but Loving Kindness was already unfolding its path to me.

For the first half of my life, I had no idea how to define Loving Kindness or how to share with others how I practiced it. From early childhood it was my natural spiritual quality. It's who I am at my core.

From my young years, I trusted life.

I grew up in a small town in the midwest during an age where there was time for friendship, swimming in the big town pool, bike riding and summer trips to the northwoods of Wisconsin.

I could leave for hours and not tell my parents where I was going and there was no cause for alarm.

I loved going to church. I was mesmerized by pictures of Jesus. Being in church made me feel part of a larger love. Also, the rituals of church were meaningful to me. The candle lighting, the incense and the costumes of the clergy. Inside that small world I conjured all sorts of fantasies about life.

I loved spending time in my Grandpa's cabin in the northwoods of Wisconsin. The thick forests contained great mysteries to be uncovered. Large mossy patches underneath trees, wild berries, wild mint, flora and fauna. I could wander for long periods in these woods. Or just sit alone and be quiet, listening to my breath and the sounds within the woods. There was a beautiful clean lake where we spent countless hours fishing, water skiing, and catching crabs. Near the shoreline there was a pine woods and a lakeside hammock that hung sleepily beneath two tall fluffy white pine trees. Here I was golden. I had freedom to roam and fill into my life.

My childhood was full of all of the time in the world. I lived a life in slow motion that had plenty of room for cultivating the practice of

Loving Kindness. It would not be until much later that I knew to call it that, but when I was taking meditative walks in the woods as a ten year old girl, that's exactly what I was doing.

Everything changed for me when I experienced the heartbreak of my parents' divorce at the age of twelve. This late childhood event brought my first struggle with trust and doubt. I stopped feeling safe. I was exposed suddenly to how love ends, and to how things we thought were permanent can shatter into a million pieces.

The disruption of childhood is something that we all experience in different ways and with varying intensities. Disruptions come in the form of traumas like divorce, deaths or abuse and they come in the form of more subtle realizations that the world is full of suffering, unfair or unsafe in some way.

My childhood disruption placed me on a path of trying to figure out how to deal with my intense emotions and deepest fears. I believe that these significant childhood experiences can teach us how to open our hearts to others who have suffered.

I have revisited this family-of-origin wound all of my adult life, but it was a gift to my own growth as a human. I was drawn to Loving Kindness while working through my sadness and frustrations early in life. I became a caretaker at a young age of the others in my family who were hurting. Out of this grew a deep compassion for the common human struggle.

And Loving Kindness grows out of compassion. The deeply sensitive five year old in me found her way back to Loving Kindness as a twelve year old by staying present and compassionate.

This was the journey I was born into, and though I have experienced seasons of feeling undeserving of true love and wellness, I continually return to own for myself what I want others to have, which is the path of Loving Kindness.

I believe we can all find a way through the darkness back to the light. It's daily work and worth every moment of effort. It's ever evolving work that is never complete.

I've evolved through many struggles along my path. What makes me a guide and a healer is that I live my story of healing every day. It's because of my own journey that I am able to help others. I'm able to be present for other people and be their witness. I can see them. All of our stories are similar.

Meditation

FOR BRINGING LOVING KINDNESS TO YOUR DISRUPTED CHILDHOOD:

Go to your spot for meditation. Whether it's a chair or a mat or a blanket on the floor, I find it helpful to always use the same spot. If you like, you can have a candle you light to begin or just place your hands with your palms open on your knees or thighs to signal that your practice has begun.

Read the meditation below a few times and then close your eyes for 5-10 minutes while you meditate. Afterwards spend about five more minutes answering the journal questions below.

Meditation

Some people might say I'm a Loving Kindness activist, but I know the seeds of this activism were with me as I held space for the nationwide tragedy of the death of JFK and for my family as we experienced together the suffering caused by our family's fragmentation. In the meditation below, I want to hold space for the suffering you experienced as a child.

Begin by stating your intention. All of us experience some kind of loss of innocence in our childhood. As you meditate, can you hold yourself a container of Loving Kindness for the ways in which your childhood was disrupted? Whatever comes up for you, can you observe yourself as a child and bring Loving Kindness to that situation. Spend about ten minutes loving the child that you were in those situations. Remain free from judging any thoughts you have. Just observe with a container of love.

After you spend a few minutes meditating, take some time to journal about your experience.

Journaling Questions

What are one or two of your major childhood disruptions?

Journaling Questions

What did it look like to love yourself as a child in the meditation practice?

Broken Hearts Grow Beautiful New Things

A wise woman wishes to be no one's enemy;
a wise woman refuses to be anyone's victim.

Maya Angelou

My journey into a conscious practice of Loving Kindness began when I realized that I was suffering repeatedly with the same themes and patterns. Like most women, I was very hard on myself. I was not able to hear my own voice or know my own callings. I had a strong desire to really know myself from the inside out and to not be so caught up in our culture's ideal images of what the good life should be.

But also like most women, there were places in my life and parts of my soul that I struggled to love.

Loving Kindness practice can sound so simple or even trite when talking about it in theory. And like I said earlier, we can all mentally agree whenever we hear someone talking about practicing self-love.

But often in practice we are actually only loving ourselves when we feel we deserve it or when we feel we have achieved some kind of success. When we feel proud of ourselves, we might allow ourselves to experience a small inward gaze of love. Sometimes we only love a version of ourselves that we are projecting, the person that we have created in our minds that we hope to be, not the person that we actually are.

Where the rubber meets the road is when we experience failure or disappointment. True Loving Kindness means loving ourselves when we are most tempted to direct at ourselves a gaze of self-loathing instead of self-loving.

The moments of darker truth and places of deep suffering are where I learned how my Loving Kindness practice is not just airy words. Loving Kindness would help me cope with my most intense losses. It helped me love the parts of myself I did not want to face.

Like many young women, I entered and experienced relationships without understanding that we can't make another happy if we aren't happy. And of course, we can't be happy unless we love ourselves.

I spent years trying to make everyone else happy and denying my own unhappiness.

This is exactly the opposite of self-love. I had a long road ahead of me towards a true understanding of Loving Kindness.

I didn't want to hurt anyone. I was willing to let myself suffer so that others didn't have to.

But this kind of martyrdom is not true love for others. I could not offer to others what I did not have myself.

Facing my own unhappiness and the fact that I was failing in my attempts to make those around me happy took me to a dark place of shame and sadness.

Mercifully, rock bottom is often the place where we can find Loving Kindness.

When everything we have tried is no longer working or when all of our methods of coping and hiding are clearly not giving us the results we desire, we have a window of openness to try something different. This is where Loving Kindness befriended me.

Through Loving Kindness I learned to forgive myself for ways I had harmed others. Soon my practice of Loving Kindness even taught me how to forgive those who harmed me.

When my darkest days were behind me, I knew that I didn't want to return to a life of not loving myself.

I was curious about how to live a life that felt more like me.

I wanted to be more intentional about my numbered days and to live with more appreciation and inner calm. Peace of mind became my number one aspiration.

I returned again and again to loving myself, then to loving others and loving the world. This is the cycle of Loving Kindness. It taught me to know and see the ways I had kept my mind small and narrow. It taught me to empathize with another person's struggle, to be gentle when dealing with negative people, difficult people, or hard situations.

Loving Kindness became my spiritual quality. I would be lost without it. And actually it has always been within me, as it is also within you. We go through seasons and even years of self-forgetting, but Loving Kindness is there waiting.

When your heart breaks, you will find Loving Kindness a willing companion.

You can allow it to grow.

A Meditation
FOR DARK DAYS
AND BROKEN HEARTS:

I have a method I've developed over the years when the going gets rough.

It's become a sacred practice to me.

When I'm triggered, I sit down on the ground and give myself a few minutes before I respond.

I sit and I breathe and I wait.

I experience silence. I'm not doing, I'm just there.

I wait.

The silence is my friend.

Silence is a gift.

Inside the silence, is where the seed of compassion grows.

Practice this way of being.

It's not a guarantee that no pain or suffering will be in your life.

This way of pausing is a doorway to feeling tender loving care for your own process, for finding a way through.

Stay soft dear hearts.

Journaling Questions

Journal about where you have seen Loving Kindness befriend you during hard times.

Journaling Questions

Coming Home to Mama Italy

What is the fatal charm of Italy?
What do we find there that can be found nowhere else?
I believe it is a certain permission to be human, which other places, other countries, lost long ago.

Erica Jong

Just as Loving Kindness especially befriends us during the darkest seasons of our lives, it also takes our hand to dance with us in the most exquisite moments of our lives.

For me, the explosions of Loving Kindness I have experienced in Italy have been ecstasy.

I knew on that day in the library as a young mother that I would one day visit Italy. I had already felt its call on my heart. I was drawn to a country that is thousands of years deep, and no other place would do. I wanted to feel the heart of Italy from the inside out.

I went to Italy seeking a spiritual mentor. I had no idea it would be an entire country.

I came to Italy for the first time in my late thirties. Like many first time visitors, my first trip was too busy and hurried. It was a typical see-it-all tour and I longed to slow it all down, to be in Mama Italy in slow time. My destiny would be to return again and again, to let her nourish me with her easy pace of life.

But even on that hurried trip, from my first steps onto Italian soil, I was all in. My entire being felt home at last. It was an ancient call in present time, and no words can accurately describe the sense that stunned my soul. Many healers, psychics, and medicine people have told me that I've lived many lifetimes in Italy. Possibly, I even sat as a nun through ancient times. In Italy, I was waking up to my authentic self.

After years of taking care of others, Italy took me in her arms and invited me to soften my heart and live with more self-love, *amore per se stessi*.

La Belleza, the beauty of Italy, collided with my spiritual longing and a fire was ignited from the inside out. So deeply moving was the spirit of the Italian people, the history and meaning of the food, the intentional celebration of life itself, and the gorgeous magic within every ancient hill town.

I wasn't interested in conquering Italy. My plan was to slowly meander through it, returning often as though it was a long lost friend.

I prefer getting real when I travel, connecting to the earthy essence of the place. Instead of attempting to see every museum or recommended tourist site, I want to take in the smells, the flavors and the daily life of the people who live there. I arrive in Italy with an open mind and a strong curiosity about learning how other people live. I treasure the times spent in slow conversation or just trying to dive deeper into understanding Italian!

On my last visit I stayed at a quaint agriturismo near where my retreat would begin just a few days later. My luggage was lost and I was jet lagged, but those things didn't even matter because here I was in this heavenly place with the kindest, most caring innkeepers. A young couple so full of life, and willing to make sure all of my needs were met. It was almost too much for me to take. They delivered beautiful food to my room, a robe and some toiletries, a glass of *vino*. That night in my Tuscan bedroom positioned just next to an olive grove, a gentle rain and wind swept through the land. I left the windows open. It will go down in history as one of the most amazing nights of sleep I ever had in adulthood. Thirteen hours where I barely moved, and a couple times woke to a gentle whooshing of the olive branches and the sweet smell of fresh rain.

It's those really human interactions that matter so much. Of all the glorious and stunning things I saw on that trip, months later I'm still smiling about how lovingly cared for I was at that simple dwelling in the Tuscan countryside. These are the Italian memories that will stick forever.

Italy has uncovered all the ways I want to connect deeper with life. There is a saying in Italy which is, *Il Dolce Far Niente*, and it means the sweetness of doing nothing. This way of being is how we can be present and savor the very essence and gift of our humanity.

To practice the sweetness of doing nothing seems a very tall order given the way most of us move through our days, years, and lives. We live with a daily sense of speed and anxiety that is unprecedented. Driven by our changing economy, political climate, and rapidly evolving society, we feel we can never catch up. We have a very tough time paying attention because there is too much to pay attention to. We are constantly faced with decisions which create more anxiety and stress. Science shows that our brains do have the ability to process all the information we take in, but at a cost. Sleep disorders, digestive issues, depression, and alienation have become societal norms.

So how can we be more present in our lives with so much to contend with? How can we savor life with less daily stress and more joy? How can we be more like Italians?

Life is beautiful and fragile. We have moments of knowing this fragility when a loved one dies or when we experience something unexpected. But for the most part we opt out of the reality of how short life is. We escape pain with alcohol, drugs, food, sex, shopping, anger or screens. We are sleepwalking through life.

In Italy I had the breathtaking realization that not everyone in the world lives this way. On my journeys through Tuscany and small towns, on my trips to vineyards and farms, I saw people who were fully awake to life.

During my first trips to Italy I was hearing deeper voices inside my consciousness telling me that I was not living in the moment as much as I wanted to. I was practicing healthy eating, moving my body, meditating and asana, yet I still felt off.

Something was calling to me about basic pleasure. Was I feeling enough pleasure? And what about joy? What about the simplicity and beauty of joy? I wanted to spend time understanding what that meant for me. I didn't want to take another workshop, read another book or talk to a therapist. I wanted to figure it out amongst the beingness I craved as I sat and observed village life in Tuscany. There I saw how time slowed way down and people took great care to communicate with each other soulfully. Everyone was present. I was watching Loving Kindness in action. I noticed that very old people were out and about. They were working in restaurants or walking down the street with a friend or grandchild. They were sauntering about, comfortable in their own space. They weren't tucked away neatly in a nursing home waiting to die.

Observing all of this made me feel lonely for my own life. I wanted something else. Italy has been my muse for discovering what that "something" else was.

I started visiting quiet and tucked away places in Italy. I met vineyard owners. I met keepers of olive groves and makers of olive oil. I spoke with cheese artisans and passionate chefs.

Italy is a dizzying array of energy, sights, sounds and gastronomic experiences. Its beauty can be crushing. I had to learn how to sit down and be fully present. Italy is very loving, giving and generous but it wants you to give too, to surrender to the possibilities and experience the expansion. So many times in Italy, I have had to let go of what I thought I wanted, in order to experience what is. That surrender is part of tapping into Italy's magic.

I'll admit I'm a bit of an idealist, a dreamer and I love to dwell in the realm of possibility about how life can be more beautiful, more loving, with more happy moments. I'm sure in a former life I was a poet in 15th century Venice, Italy wearing long shimmery gowns, gazing at beautiful art and listening to baroque music.

Italy feels like a return to my original self. I felt that way the first time I laid eyes on the ceiling of the *Cappella Sistina*. I knew it when I swam in the Mediterranean Sea and heard the Italians laughing. Each moment in Italy is a sigh of relief, *I'm home*. In Italy I learned profoundly rich lessons about how to see *La Belleza* (the beauty) of the world, and stay devoted to *Amore Volezza*, Loving Kindness.

Soon, my Loving Kindness path led me to begin to share Italy with others by hosting restorative retreats marked by *La Dolce Vita*. Bringing people to the smaller towns and villages of Italy where they can experience this slow pace and take in *Bella Italia* in deep time has been my unique way of loving the world.

It was not a seamless process. Over the years I have had to learn a great deal about bridging the gap between being a yoga teacher and a retreat host. I have had to let go of some plans, improvise new plans and stay in my rested, loving self. But even when everything shifts and plans have to change, I have multiple moments while leading retreats in Italy where I have overwhelming joy and think, "I can't believe this is happening."

Changing weather or changing moods can create madcap moments of scrambling, much like putting on a live show every day. So much beauty and experience can be hard to take in, so I try to give my yoga classes a rooted sensation, a gentle container for travelers who are experiencing so much stimulation.

On my retreats I love to take people off the beaten path. We don't do touristy things. I've discovered authentic experiences that are affordable, with fabulous food, loving people and a beautiful nurturing environment. I prefer to find places that have charm and substance where the stories of the owners match the beauty of the land. It's slow flow travel. We have our ups and downs but it's real. People make lasting friendships. They learn about their capacity to grow. I always tell my retreaters that you have to dive in! Don't just sit still wondering what it would be like. Go for it.

My retreat groups are diverse and full of human struggle, so it is fascinating when they all come together. We tend to live in a fairly isolating or private lifestyle, but we need tribe and communing. We need to be with people in order to feel belonging and we may resist one another based on our personalities, but being together teaches us so much about our true nature. It is always fascinating to witness how people can draw together to help, to encourage, to hold space for one another and to share their humanity. I think this happens partly because the Italian people who host us offer such open hospitality. My experience has been that they care for us so well and are patient with us needy Americans. They always have time for us.

The people I have met at the castles, vineyards and villas where I have hosted yoga retreats have showed me how to be willingly present to others. They offered their services to us with grace.

And when everything works, the guests are able to surrender to that grace. They are free to create a true Sangha, a beautiful community.

Once I was sitting on a hill overlooking the *Val D'Orcia* while leading a retreat for fifteen soul seekers. Everyone was at their own level. I always find it fascinating to learn so much about the human condition as it relates to what resonates for each person. It was a windy day blowing kisses of peace to our group. I had just finished teaching a yoga class and everyone was in deep relaxation after a slow purposeful journey through asana. The sun was shining down in a way that opened up every possibility for Loving Kindness. It was one of those generous moments in time when awakened energy and feelings of peace were present. Many times while teaching I've had tears well up as I sit with my students at the end of class. There is such an innocence in seeing how vulnerable we are as humans in our bodies, our spirits, the moments. It's a time of joy for me. I feel how similar all of us are. We all want the same things really. Love, joy, peace of mind.

That day, I sat quietly reflecting on twenty years of teaching yoga. I felt so grateful for my good fortune as a teacher, and for how my path had led me to Tuscany.

My experience in leading retreats in Italy is so vast and open that at times it seems like I might just float up into the clouds. Whether it's leading a class on the edge a vineyard, gathering around tables laden with local cheese and wine, watching Americans learn to roll out homemade pasta from an Italian grandma or leading groups through ancient hilltowns, being in Italy is the ultimate celebration of life, trusting in the present moment and in nature itself.

The Italians have a profound way of living daily with what they call *amore della vita*, which is a love of life. Their late afternoon or evening routine of strolling through the piazza on a *Passeggiata* is how they celebrate life itself without pause. To be in the very moments of life with joyful presence is a far cry from our relentless pursuit of success or of a life driven by work. It's no contest which of those I prefer, but I had to go to Italy to learn how to practice loving life and being present in this ancient way.

Italy Travel Notes

Dear heart, I offer you a few notes from my travel diaries and a list of my favorite places that might assist you on your own pilgrimage home to Mama Italy. A word of warning: Italy by nature is feminine and sensuous. She enchants you if you are willing. Do not resist. Resistance will only haunt you later.

Visit ancient hilltowns. Every hilltown I've explored in Tuscany has its own smell, light and sensation. Walk around and enjoy the sight of fresh flowers and street life, taste the food and wine and smell the aged *percorino* (cheese) and leather. Enjoy the open air markets with their stunning colors of fruit, vegetables, figs, salami, cheese, and pasta. Tuscany is the heart of Italy and will possess you with postcard-perfect hilltop villages, dating back to the middle ages. Pienza, Montalcino, Montepulciano, Lucca, Arezzo, Cortona, Castelmuzio, Trequanda, Sarteano, San Gimignano are all lovingly restored and preserved. Each hilltown is within 20-40 minutes of another one, a universe unto itself. They sit elegantly in their natural habitat within rolling hillsides, cypress lined drives, farmhouses, vineyards and breathtaking iconic images.

Pienza has a unique spiritual quality and sits in the heart of Tuscany. My first trip there found me wanderlusting through the Piazzo Pio 11, embracing the spirit of ancient energies. On every corner within the square is gelato that smells like joy, pecorino cheese that has a primal air about it, and the smell of wine mixed with life. In Pienza I could sit for hours taking in the gorgeous renaissance architecture of the cathedral and the Palazzo

Piccolomini. The invitation to stay longer is ever present. I've sat for hours at a small table in Pienza overlooking the *Val d'Orcia*. Pope Pius 11 wanted to create the ideal city based on the humanist values of the time.

The road to Montepulciano is charmed with olive groves, vineyards, farms and stone houses. There is a felt sense of belonging, knowing and comfort. In the *piazza* (square) the *sacro* (sacred) Cathedral beckons. The whole town is shaped like an S with medieval walls circling around it. I found my way to Cafe Poliziano where wine and coffee have been served up since 1868. I can feel the energy of the saints and sinners who inhabited all of the hill towns. With so much art, history, food, and beauty to absorb I often end up realizing I need more time. Just a few more days, or weeks or months.

Go on a quest to San Gimignano to sample what has been dubbed the best artisan "Gelataria di Piazza" in all of Italy. Innovating with sensations like lavender, essence of rosemary, saffron and chili peppers, savor the savory is the word. On my visit, I stayed for longer than I imagined and sampled small amounts of 5 or 6 flavors. Limona is still at the top of my list. The woman behind the counter watched my face as I tasted and said, *Ah sensuale!* (sensual) Yes, eating gelato is a sensual experience. Slow down to savor.

Visit tiny Monteriggioni, encased by circular walls and fourteen preserved military towers. Steeped in history and off the beaten path, Monteriggioni is an ideal place to hang with the locals sipping on a robust cappuccino. Just outside of town I experienced one of my top ten eating experiences of all time, a sublime Italian meal at La Leggenda dei Frati. Tortellini stuffed with pigeon, lasagna made with chestnut flour and wild boar sauce with leeks and Pecorino equals bliss. After such a meal, I always need what the Italians call *riposo*, an afternoon nap.

Cortona has been beautifully highlighted by writer Frances Mayes, and it nurtured my heart also. You enter this ancient Etruscan hamlet by walking up a steep hill. On my first visit, I was greeted by two Italian *Nonna*, grandmothers, with smiles that would melt away anything unloving. Cats wandering freely, skinny and flirtatious. Again find a cafe to sit in and do nothing. Sip slowly. Stay longer, order lunch, a gorgeous platter of *pici all 'aglione*, a garlic-infused traditional Tuscan dish pumped up with gorgeous fresh manzano tomatoes, fresh hot peppers and basil.

The Tuscan countryside! Etruscan villages such as Montalcino, Pienza, Sienna and Sarteano. Sarteano is a slice of real life, quaint and off the grid. Their weekly farmers market has just about everything you need to live *la dolce vita*. A few words I wrote in my journal about this part of Tuscany: "Here is a kaleidoscope of moods, sunrises, sunsets, tuscan sun, flora and fauna, humans, vibes, foods, laughter, personalities, rituals, ancient stories, and ways of being."

Find an agriturismo to truly experience Italian life. Agriturismo is a combination of the words for "agriculture" and "tourism" in Italian. Vacationing in a farmhouse often means eating off the land, tasting organic olive oil and local wine served with dinner. Yes! Prego. Even better if you find a medieval residence, perhaps with an elegant loggia and bell tower or frescoes from the 16th century. Vineyards and villas across Tuscany rent out rooms by the week with meals included. Rent a car so you can explore nearby towns during the day and then come home each night to your piece of Mama Italy.

The beautiful Valdichiana is an excellent base opening up both the Siena region and the Umbria region around Lake Trasimeno.

With rich Etruscan history all around, any nook may hide a treasure and artistic works are found in the most surprising ways.

In Italy I believe in slow eating, slow sipping and slow walking. Anyway you can slow down will open up the possibility of being nourished by Bella Italia. When I am home in Italy, I can feel into the full measure of my hours and days. Time is deep. I feel so happy that I chuckle to myself, half embarrassed to feel this joyful. Ah, this is *la dolce vita.*

A Meditation

FOR DREAMING
OF MAMA ITALY:

Above all, I believe Italy has taught me to be present, to slow down. Where can you listen to Mama Italy for a day or a weekend (or even longer) and bring a slower way of living into your life, even if it's just for a season?

Dream of Mama Italy reaching all the way to your corner of the world and teaching you the Loving Kindness of slowing down just one piece of your day. Can you walk to work this week instead of drive? Can you stay at the table and savor a meal for longer?

Journaling Questions

Write about the experience of dreaming about Mama Italy.

Journaling Questions

Where can the practices of La Dolce Vita aid and enhance your practice of Loving Kindness?

Journaling Questions

My Journey Into

YOGA, SHAMANISM, AND LOVING KINDNESS

Yoga should not be a training for body control;
on the contrary it must bring freedom to the body.
Vanda Scaravelli

In yoga I can completely trust what's happening. The experience rests in my feelings. I'm not listening to my mind anymore. It's just the moment and it's incredibly refreshing.

I believe that how we experience our world is not through our mind but through our body. Yoga is a tender exploration, an inward path.

One of the reasons I started teaching yoga was to help make the world a better, happier place.

My belief in yoga's ability to do just that is what drove my ambition from the very beginning of teaching yoga. Now that many years have passed and I've taught hundreds and hundreds of yoga classes, that belief is even stronger.

I'm not sure balance truly exists in the definition of the word itself. I prefer to think that what really happens when we're practicing yoga is that we're having a period of alignment with soul. This can also occur when we are feeling connected to someone, living a beautiful moment, or feeling truly happy.

Those moments of alignment are often brief, but we must hold them dearly. We hold on to them and appreciate them. What we embody wholeheartedly is mysterious. True happiness might not be when we're feeling incredibly healthy, beautiful, in love, rich or any of the things that our culture tells us that we have to be in order to be happy.

It might be unplanned and random. It's almost always fleeting.

This is nature. Everything changes and passes, but we have to catch it while we can. We learn to savor and to know life as beauty or what the Italians call *La Belleza*. To know, feel it within every inch of our being.

We realize that happiness and life will show us intense shadow and light.

Loving Kindness in action means we don't reject either one. Both have much to teach us.

This lesson and practicing Loving Kindness has been the essence of my journey with yoga.

By the time I entered college I had a strong interest in health, wellness, mysticism and spiritual practices. I worked at a health food store and devoured books, knowledge and anything I could about living a holistic life. I knew that one day I would help people feel better in their body, mind and spirit. I wanted to help people learn how to love life.

I was influenced by the mystics like Thomas Moore. I loved his heart and take on the world. J. Krishnamurti is still influencing me and I use his books weekly as study guides. My first book on Buddhism was *Shambhala Sacred Path of the Warrior*, written in 1984 by Chogyam Trungpa. His teachings have influenced me the most of all Buddhist teachers. I love his rogue approach to the traditional aspects of Buddhism. His theory was to question authority and experts. To ask about what doesn't make sense. To stand up for yourself when you have something to say. And mostly to keep the dharma active in all that you do for it will relieve suffering the most.

Teaching yoga was my entry point. What I didn't realize before teaching is that being with people in the capacity of a yoga teacher is both daunting and fulfilling. In western society we are deeply habituated to forward motion. Yoga invites us to slow down and be present, which goes against the grain. So the energy that you are working with most of the time as a yoga teacher is the energy of resistance.

After graduating with a degree in health and wellness, I ended up working in corporate America for a period of time. I was working in technology right at the start of the boom, which had its benefits. It was an emerging time for the digital revolution. I enjoyed connecting and building relationships with people. Business was becoming slightly more interesting to me, although I viewed it as a boys' club where I didn't fit in. I knew this work wasn't permanent but a means to an end. Culture was shifting and creating awareness around wellness. I slowly plotted my exit strategy. The same day I quit my corporate job, I went to the print shop to order my new business cards. I called my company *Yoga by Jane* and off I went.

It was clear to me at the start that I wanted to teach Loving Kindness. I used the Buddha's teachings on impermanence, and the four noble truths as the bedrock of my philosophy.

I had an immediate sense of wanting to empower my students with self-love and strength. To be tender-hearted and physically strong was compelling. That was my early focus as a teacher. I taught an intersection of physical yoga conflated with the classical teachings on compassion. I encouraged being open and present to life with a non-judging mind.

My students were hungry for internal peace, and to understand how compassion leads to self-knowing, self-love and a kinder planet. I devoted my days to the life of yoga teacher, savoring the ephemeral moments of connection. I was learning and teaching at the speed of light. I was in my zone. I was seeking a container to place my spiritual callings, so teaching yoga became my vehicle. The teachings on compassion and Loving Kindness brought everything together. Through my experience teaching I discovered how to move people into Loving Kindness. It was astonishing to me to realize that it was mostly about giving people permission.

Yoga from the inside out was my moniker. I didn't have mirrors in my teaching studio. I told students to feel the alignment from within. I was giving permission to be without striving.

To heal the body, mind and spirit by just being tender and gentle with oneself.

I witnessed through hundreds of teaching hours that there is no greater teaching than Loving Kindness for healing.

In my view, yoga is where we come home to our bodies safely, lovingly and without aggression. It wasn't easy in the beginning years to teach from this perspective. Loving one's body is not a natural inclination for most, especially during a time when yoga was all about the body doing amazing things from the outside in. I wanted to teach my students how to embrace yoga from the inside out.

Teaching, teaching, teaching. I just kept my head down and taught. I didn't question whether I was on the right path or not. I loved the truly generous moments of teaching. I experienced how it was transformative for so many. It was a gift and an honor to be part of it.

I taught my students about Loving Kindness through asanas, meditations and readings. I witnessed how it was helping them handle their difficult emotions. There was always progress, even if it was slow. Teaching yoga requires great patience and the ability to help students stay with it. The practice is what it's all about. It's all practice. Those who were attracted to going inward were the people who were drawn to my teachings.

In what might be considered one of the most audacious moves of my adulthood, I decided to open up my own studio. I built out an old space that used to house a gay porn shop. It seemed a perfect place to imbue the teachings of Loving Kindness. I named it 360 Yoga Studio with the intention of encouraging all ages, abilities and all people to join our ever growing sangha. Centered in the heart of a trendier youthful area of Minneapolis, 360 did well soon after opening. On Saturday mornings I taught enough people and made enough money to pay all of the bills for the entire month.

360 Yoga was my life for five years, seven days a week, morning, noon and night. I lived, breathed, and slept in the studio. I made my

teaching bones there. Soon it became day in and day out. There were days of sheer exhaustion but the moment the students arrived, all was well. I was always able to step completely outside myself when I taught. I'm unsure how that skill came to me but it's never left me. I've often joked that teaching yoga has saved me from myself. When I'm teaching or practicing, all is right in the world.

The final space and build out of 360 Yoga was lovely. High ceilings of old hammered metal painted a pale soft cream and walls to match. Lighting with a star like softness tucked into the ceiling. The floors were a beautiful warm wood, glossy and inviting. Light came in through the large front windows in just the right mood. There was a small platform stage where we made an altar with a singing bowl from Tibet used daily by all teachers. Green Tara Buddha greeted everyone at the front door, a precious gift from a student named Jack who was all heart.

In the opening ceremony I invited a Buddhist nun to chant the heart sutra. There was healthy delicious food, live tablas, and vitality in the air. It was a halcyon moment. We were creating something beautiful on the spot. There wasn't a handbook for how to bring this all together. It was a creative pursuit I honed for a long time, and those skills would follow me forevermore. I've often reflected on those times as being a gift from the cosmos, a way for me to share in community, find my tribe and feel safe and whole again in the world.

I had several corporate clients, private clients, and was leading retreats in addition to teaching roughly twenty yoga classes a week. Anyone who knows anything about teaching can attest to the insanity of that schedule. What was I thinking? My body seemed to be holding up, but I was often yearning for silence. It was grueling and magnificent all at once.

The yearning for silence was a call to my deepest need for inner listening and knowing.

There are chapters in life where we heed a call. We unshackle what no longer serves us, and welcome who we're becoming.

After a while, I found that the more I taught, the more wired up I became internally. Being in community with so many like-minded souls was filling me up, then depleting me at the same time. I was making a good living as a yoga teacher and business owner. Yoga continued to explode on the scene, and I was right there at the edge of it all. It was hard to say no to those who wanted to dive in and know the practice. I just kept teaching, giving, teaching, giving.

In my heart of hearts I believed I was helping to change the world one breath at a time. My energy was in a constant state of buzz. I could sense the ripple effect classes were having on everyone who entered our doors. Stories of Loving Kindness were coming back to me. I was doing a bit of holistic life coaching in every class I taught. Unknown to me until years later, my studio was at the center of the first wave zeitgeist of yoga studios in our area.

In the early 2000s yoga had mainstream allure even though it was still in its infancy in many ways. Teachers were creating their own theories, preferences, and styles. Wall Street took notice and started to pay attention, so a version of yoga was created that could be sold and marketed to the masses. I saw the beginning of the capitalization of yoga and wellness. These days the marketing of spirituality for a happier life is in full bloom.

But at 360 Yoga, all of the students who attended classes felt the blessings of our sangha. It was powerful and affirming beyond measure. It was a unique moment in time, never to be repeated, always to be cherished.

My teaching schedule was continually growing. Through those years of running the studio, I took a few vacations hoping to replenish and rest. But even while I was gone, I was concerned about the studio, in touch with the instructors, wanting to make sure our little haven was unharmed. I had a tough time turning it off.

After years of non-stop, I was beginning to feel overwhelmed emotionally, physically and mentally. The closer I got to other people's hearts through teaching, the more my own heart opened. To touch into the essence of people in that way is both beautiful and exhausting. Even with good boundaries it's quite challenging to process.

Being the boss of a yoga studio gave me authority, yet with that authority was a growing fear of showing any signs of weakness. My own practice of yoga and meditation was not sustaining me at that point. The irony of that is not subtle. The more my business grew, the less I had time to practice. At the same time, I was supposed to model a radiant being who was untouched by stress.

No one was pushing me to work that hard. It was fully my choice to live this way, but I reached a point where I recognized that I was becoming a prisoner to my own success and something had to change.

To alleviate some of my own exhaustion and suffering, I decided to take a slight detour from the world of yoga and study with a shaman. I was reading the book *The Way of the Shaman*, and my interest was piqued. I was particularly interested in the Q'ero tribe after learning about their long history of teaching love and kindness.

The Q'ero are the last of the Incas who lived in virtual solitude until they were discovered in 1949 by Dr. Alberto Villoldo. They believe that "munay," love and compassion, will be the guiding force of this *great gathering of the peoples.*

The teaching of the Q'ero:
Follow your own footsteps.
Learn from the rivers,
The trees and the rocks.
Honor the Christ,
The Buddha,
Your brothers and sisters.
Honor the Earth Mother and the Great Spirit.
Honor yourself and all of creation.
Look with the eyes of your soul and engage the essential.

I heard about a guy living in Minneapolis who apprenticed with the Q'ero Inca shamans in Peru. He was now practicing shamanism and offering sessions called soul retrievals. A soul retrieval returns lost parts of our soul which we can lose through life traumas or spiritual illness. The moment was right. This kind of healing intrigued me so I booked a session for October 31.

If you're going to do a soul retrieval, why not Halloween?

Steve Haney was a large framed ex-football player with a magnetic smile and slightly mischievous presence. He was both earthy and imbued with spiritual resonance. Being in his presence was immediately comforting. Within moments of our first meeting I knew I had found my next teacher.

On Halloween night in 2004, I entered the studio to his workspace, walking up a long flight of creaky old stairs in a vintage two story in uptown Minneapolis. The night was warm and windy. There was a glimmer of enchantment in the air. I felt a bit intrepid with a shot of humility.

We had a long conversation over the phone before our first session in which Steve explained what a soul retrieval was. We were basically going to soul dive into the depths of my being to bring back parts of my soul that were stolen, missing, or wounded. I'll admit I felt both skeptical and giddy at the possibility.

The energy of Steve and his work is massive. He is at once alarming in his physical stature and calming like a gentle giant. I immediately felt safe in his space and energy.

After a brief conversation where Steve asked me about significant themes and life events, he instructed me to lie down on a massage table face up. The candlelit room was peaceful. It was quiet enough to hear the wind blowing through the trees outside, as well as the leaves crisply touching the ground. The room was warm and imbued with softness. Steve sat down on a chair right next to the end of the table where my head was. He held my right hand between both of his hands. That act alone brought me into a place of intense joy. To be witnessed and to journey this way was life changing. I felt safe in the holy space. Steve told me we were going to get quiet and focus on deep breathing. His instructions were clear and direct. I was able to fully relax my body. I was so tired that I wondered if I would drift off to sleep. I felt like I could let down my guard and just be. What a sweet relief after all these years of being up front.

Then after a period of time I literally felt electricity vibrating from his hands to my hand that he was holding, then into my entire body. It's hard to completely explain the physical sensation of this event. I was fully awake, utterly softened, and spiritually attuned to something deep inside my soul. Then I had a vision. I saw myself as a young girl. I was sad and not at all happy. Sitting alone brooding. At that exact moment Steve said to me, "Why don't you tell Jane that it's ok for her to have more fun. She can be less serious, less concerned about how everyone else is doing."

What? How did he know what my vision was? I didn't tell him.

We didn't share words at all up to that point. But he knew exactly what was happening in my mind. He went on to give young Jane a blessing and call back to my present self. He invited her to come back and safely be united with me. I could literally feel the transference of energy. The electricity heightened and then the tears came. I am not much of a crier, but I began to weep profoundly. For a long time, I was unconcerned with anything else but that moment and that experience. I was fully present for the healing.

Then I was instructed to breathe gently for a while, slowly come back to the outside world. Steve told me what he saw in his vision. That young Jane became way too serious in early childhood. She was fully aware of adults and their struggles emotionally. I had hooked into those struggles and needed to unhook from them for my own well being. It was time to not be so hard on myself, to learn how to experience more joy and more pleasure in my life.

The brilliance of that session with Steve Haney has never left my heart. Our work together brought to the surface a life-long theme of overfunctioning to get my needs met. Little did I know that I would continuously have to revisit this topic and do some intense healing for much of my adult life.

Steve was both humble and incredibly strong. He maintained a joyful countenance even though he suffered with intense physical pain. He had an accident at one point in life that severely injured his hip. He had many surgeries, many complications. His health suffered immensely from this accident as the years went on, but he still kept smiling and doing good work in the world. He loved his children and family. When I asked him in 2011 to perform my marriage ceremony he was honored. He took it very seriously and wore a beautiful suit. He practiced and prepared as though it was the royal wedding. It was one of the happiest days of my life as he stood there giving his blessings to my marriage.

For ten years after that first session, I met with Steve several times a year to engage in practices of shamanism. In my studies with Steve, I learned teachings on Loving Kindness within the foundation practices of Q'ero Inca shamanism. The focus of my mentorship was to explore who I really am on a soul level. To establish a healthy relationship within myself and my energetic relationships with others. Inca focuses on strong ties with mama earth, nature, and the stars to open our heart, cleanse the body, realize our inner vision and clear old toxic patterns.

The Q'ero believe that the seed of light was planted in our heart and soul at the moment of our birth. It is connected to our inner child, known as the Inca seed. For many humans, the seed will lie dormant until a time where it becomes activated and nurtured. Once this seed is supported one can come back to themselves wholeheartedly. The higher purpose is to align with our work in the world on the highest level, and to experience the truest pleasures of life.

Steve taught me how to prepare and create Despachos, which are offerings of flowers and key elements given to earth in the form of a mandala. They are a way of giving thanks, honoring our relationship with abundance and healing. We also practiced many hours of tree healing, illumination light healing and many energetic clearings. These times spent in mentorship could fill a whole book. The most relevant thing I learned from Steve is how to understand my own nature in relation to those I encounter in this lifetime. How compassion in action means to cherish my own heart first, then offer compassion to others, in service to creating a more sane and kind world. It's not easy to maintain this level of higher consciousness on the daily. But it is my continuing aspiration and what I believe in with all of my being.

Steve left earth on September 16, 2015. I didn't know until three weeks after his death. He died quickly and without pain. He was 59. At the moment of his death, I was in Italy hosting my first retreat in Tuscany at an ancient castle. It was eclipse season. On the day that Steve died, I felt off. Something felt wrong in the world is what I wrote in my journal that day. That sense was followed later in the day by peace and calm. Like energy had passed through.

I believe that when Steve left, I felt it and was terrified. A true life anchor and teacher of mine, someone I trusted and respected, who married my husband and I, was no longer going to be there for me.

The calm came later that day. Somewhere inside I knew that all he taught me would forever carry me. I now had to go forward and be brave and strong and vulnerable. That is what Steve was. He never complained. He only ever gave love and wisdom. And now those beautiful teachings from the ancient Q'ero are a part of who I am, all because of Steve.

A Yoga Meditation:

Dear hearts,

Yoga is a practice where we can return to love. We can rest our weariness and take refuge.

There is no need to push, strive or achieve. It's a place for our mind to settle and know its true essence which is joy. Yoga heals our body from the inside out. Each pose and breath creates internal cleansing and awareness about how to live in our bodies safely.

Our body works so hard every day. It's always there for us, no matter what. We rely on it to take us through this world.

Our body is a miracle, something to behold.

In yoga we can tenderly ask our body what it needs and offer our deepest intentions for radiance and vitality.

Dear Body,

Thank you for being here for me every moment of my life.

We've walked a long journey together and I appreciate you with all my heart.

I want to cherish and honor our time together.

I know that you are wise beyond what I can imagine.

Today I ask you dear body, what do you need?

What do you need for rest, nourishment, connection and love?

How can I give you what you need right here and now?

Journaling Questions

What was your first encounter with yoga?

How would you describe the first time you practiced?

What parts of yoga immediately resonated with you?

Journaling Questions

How does your practice now compare to when you first began?

Where would you love to see your practice grow or deepen?

New York Sangha

I meditate so that my mind cannot complicate my life.
Sri Chinmoy

It was May 26, 2000. I opened a small note that read, "Be there at 7."

Cyndi Lee handed me the note after I attended one of her clever sessions at OM Yoga Studio New York City. Cyndi just had a way of making yoga feel like a dear old friend. Even when she taught us how to do handstands, it was sort of casual like, "come on, hands on the floor, legs up the wall, no biggie." Her method of teaching yoga was just where I wanted to be. The atmosphere at OM yoga was hipster and casual. Mats touching each other, very crowded, no place to hide. We always get the teachings we need, right?

During class she read a beautiful passage from the book *Cave in Snow* by Tenzin Palmo. After class I shared with Cyndi how much I loved the reading. Passionate about the book, she was thrilled to share with me that Tenzin was speaking at her Sangha on that very night.

Serendipity.

She invited me to join. I was completely thrilled and played it cool, "Um, Yes, I think I can make it," I said.

I took a rainy night cab ride. It was one of those NYC moments where everything felt like it was coming together. My life felt expansive. The charm and heart of that city is unmatched. Gliding along in the cab, I watched twinkly lights reflected in the puddles on the streets on my way to an unforgettable evening. Before I entered the space, I knew that my being there was divine timing.

Cave in Snow is a riveting account of how Tenzin Palmo joins a Buddhist order, then spends twelve years in a cave, in a meditation box for fifteen hours a day. Huh? Yes she did. She had food and water brought to her once a day.

This book was a game changer for me. It remains one of my top ten visionary books that has made a profound difference in how I view my ability to get down to practice. In this book I learned that it's all practice in essence. This book both kicked my butt and brought me to a softer place.

I was more than intrigued.

She gracefully entered the room, sat on her cushion which was elevated on a small podium and began her talk. A slight woman with a permanent grin. I was immediately absorbed and so was everyone else in the room. I had the deepest sense of being home. Totally embraced. Right where I needed to be. She offered the environment to let our hearts be tender. To break from the harsh outside world. It was like sweet relief.

The most engaging aspect about Tenzin was how elegant and humorous she was. She is someone you want to meditate and have tea with, but also someone you want to sit down over a couple glasses of wine with. Her ability to hold space for your heart was palpable. And there was something about joy that surrounded her. She had an aura of joy. Immediately I could sense her heart of gold.

Her vision was clear. She knows what humanity needs to help end their suffering. She spoke images straight to my heart and liberated some of the worst shackles of my mind and thought structure, and all within a two-hour talk. It made complete sense. I had this odd sense of returning to something ancient and already known deep within me. It was new but it wasn't.

Her talk was like a magic capsule and elixir for my thirsty being. Everything she said clicked. She spoke of humanity and longing. Desire and suffering. It was the beginning of a long period of deepening Svadhyaya, or self-study. Who am I, really?

Let me circle back for a moment. The cab dropped me off at the Sangha. I entered the space and it was packed. As I looked around the room I saw every sort of person. Lively conversations and a palpable feeling of happiness. It was a smallish room with over one hundred people mostly sitting on cushions, meditation style, and some on chairs. It was a warm evening on the second floor of a poorly ventilated space, stuffy and humid. No one seemed to notice or mind.

Cyndi waved me over to sit down next to her. I scrambled over and snuggled into my metal folding chair. I remember how she was a perfect balance of both poised and completely at ease. She engaged me in conversation that was right up my alley, no small talk. I've never been good at small talk so I was giddy to find a kindred spirit.

We chatted a bit before she waved to someone else to tell them to come and sit with us.

I looked up to see that Richard Gere, the actor, was coming to sit down next to Cyndi and me. In fact, he plunked down right next to me and Cyndi introduced him as a "buddy of hers." She was highly amused watching my reaction.

I was staying cool, or at least pretending to stay cool. Richard gave me a big hug and slapped me on the knee like we were long lost friends. Deep breaths in and out. The surprising aspect of that moment is how much warmth and love was buzzing around that room. The vibe was authentic. The celebrity thing just kind of didn't exist. I was sitting next to Richard Gere listening to a life changing talk.

Obviously he was very comfortable in this sangha and so was everyone else. This was the most precious thing to me. Here is this guy who is a legendary actor and superstar, loved by millions all over the world, sitting down and letting fame take a back seat.

Never mind what happens outside this sangha but in here everyone was equal, and the moments were real. I wondered if maybe this is how we know when transformation is happening in the here and now. For me I've often noticed that I don't realize transformation until after a thing has shifted or changed. It takes time for me to feel my way into it, and for it to fully blossom. But right there, in that sangha on a rainy NYC night is when I felt the power of these teachings, in this context. I still long to be back there. I think we all crave to commune in those spaces, places where we feel the most of who we are. To be able to know our self comfortably and to be assured that we're on the right path. To feel it from the inside out.

I've had very few experiences that came close to that one. For what I've come to realize since that enchanting night is that there are experiences that become the "before and after" moments of our lives. We spend so much time seeking and doubting love and life, that when we're actually in our own zone of Loving Kindness it's utterly replenishing and energizing.

This is where my own Loving Kindness practice became part of my being, never to be changed.

Tenzin's talk and teaching became my mantra for years. The way she taught, experienced and approached Loving Kindness was something I never questioned. She taught how it's the core of who we are, it's our birthright to live in the spirit of Loving Kindness. I didn't need proof or validation to know that she was brilliant and her teachings on being present were of the highest wisdom. For me to encounter her at this time on my spiritual path was written in the stars.

I ended up going back to that sangha many times over the years, taking courses and studying with a variety of teachers. It will always be a spiritual home for me.

A Meditation

FOR REMEMBERING YOURSELF:

Think of a time where you have felt the most of who you are, when you felt most connected to yourself.

Take as much time as you need. Maybe a spiritual home of your own comes to mind immediately or maybe it will take several moments of looking within yourself to remember one or two moments you experienced the fullness of Loving Kindness.

Remember as much as you can about those moments. What do you smell and see? What are the colors? What do you feel? Who is there?

Return to that space of knowing yourself. And know that you can return to that moment whenever you need it, because it is within you.

Journaling Questions

Can you identify the "before and after" moments of your life? Write them down if you can.

Journaling Questions

Or write any reflections you have from the meditation practice.

Part Three:

THE PRACTICES OF LOVING KINDNESS

Practicing Loving Kindness

*Like a caring mother holding
and guarding the life of her only child,
so with a boundless heart of loving kindness,
hold yourself and all beings as your beloved children.*
Buddha

Self-love practice is an aspiration that we make peace with our precious life so that we can live with more harmony. To have peace of mind lends itself to more feelings of happiness in all areas of life. As with many endeavors, aspiration and practice are two different animals. We all aspire to have peace. We wish and hope for it, but we don't give ourselves the space to practice. I've witnessed time and again in my own life that Loving Kindness is the practice of a lifetime. It's never too late to practice. Loving Kindness is not like your to do list. There is always time. When you are ready to move from aspiring to have peace to practicing peace, you will experience the mysterious gifts of Loving Kindness. The practice requires us to sit right down where we are now and see what's going on. It's almost absurd in its simplicity, which is perhaps why it's easy for us to go for years without doing it.

The suggestions I offer for practice should not become duties or drudgery. Beginning should feel simple. Offering yourself love. Use the meditations at the end of the beginning chapters first. Then as you dig into these practices, you can be gentle with yourself. Let these practices call to you and watch your practice of Loving Kindness grow. When you feel shaky or lost, always come back to compassion. Loving Kindness always begins with offering love to yourself.

Creating Expansive Space

*I have come to believe that caring for myself
is not self indulgent. Caring for myself is an act of survival.*

Audre Lorde

Creating space may not sound like a practice, but it absolutely is, especially in the age we live in.

Deeply embedded in our culture and way of being is the profound need to produce, move forward and compete to make our way to a successful happy life. Living this way is so common and habitual that we don't always know how deeply entrenched we are. We have been wired to think that we are supposed to be busy and tired, so it's going to take a huge shift in awareness to bring us back to wholeness.

We have short attention spans. We're receiving data at the speed of light with no way of being able to process and digest it all. Anxiety related disorders are on the rise. It's affecting our ability to sleep, digest food, be present and feel more joy.

We're moving too fast, not taking time to slow down and

appreciate what is happening moment to moment, and sooner or later we crash. You've seen it in your own life and witnessed it in others.

The entire self-care movement has been born out of the very real threat that our current way of living has on our bodies, minds and spirits.

Give yourself permission to take a stand for your own well being. Creating space is making your self-care your main priority and a daily conversation you have with yourself. The level of stress and anxiety that many humans live with is not ok, and should no longer be brushed to the side. Our way of living is not sustainable under circumstances where we don't get our spiritual, physical and emotional needs met.

We need to deepen our conversations about selfishness and what it really means. If it means I care about me and will take care of me so that I can be good for others in my life, YES! Please be selfish. If it means taking an area of your home and creating a physical reminder and space to practice in, so be it. Let the intention of setting a tone for practice guide you toward creating a space that works for you.

This is self-love and compassion in action. To live with the intention of wanting what is best for yourself so that you can be your best for others is an act of radical love.

Curating space where Loving Kindness can live and breathe requires a bit of personal care activism. In a culture that is impatient and wants it all right now, sacrifices will have to be made. Things that drain our energy have to be reconsidered.

Make a list of everything that takes up your time. Circle the things that are life-giving. Underline the things that are not. In order to actually create new habits and shifts in behaviors, we need space. Not all at once, but step by step, day by day, moment by moment.

What can you remove from your life to make space? What do you want more of in your life?

Write those two questions down on the back of your list and let them remain in your consciousness for a few days. Come back to your list again and again, and always remember that life is constantly changing. Old things can be released when they have served their purpose or are draining your energy. New things can grow in their place.

Time is perhaps the greatest gift you can give yourself as you deepen your practice of Loving Kindness.

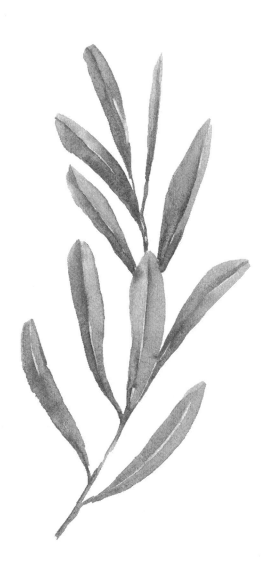

Meditation

*Our life is an endless journey; it is like a broad highway
that extends infinitely into the distance. The practice of
meditation provides a vehicle to travel on that road.
Our journey consists of constant ups and downs...
Chogyam Trungpa*

Everywhere we turn we are hearing about what an essential thing it is to meditate. You may have tried to meditate or you might already have a regular practice. Maybe you dream of a regular practice. Perhaps meditation is frustrating at times. You're not feeling it, or it's not clicking.

When we consider how our culture is all about getting ahead, striving for more, push and more push, it's no wonder that it's difficult to cultivate presence through meditation.

The Buddhist tradition of meditation is based on the premise that when we sit still, and practice breathing and maybe counting to ten, we'll eventually grow into a practice that gives us meaning.

For many years I've sampled the landscape of meditation

techniques, and learned that there is not one size fits all when it comes to meditation.

I encourage you to remember that all of the original Buddhist and Zen traditions were taught by men, for men. There are good reasons to believe that our resistance to meditation is because we are still trying to fit into an old model that doesn't serve the emerging feminine nor our collective need to soften, and live a more tenderhearted life.

We need more tools to awaken and cultivate presence, embrace both our strong and vulnerable side, and wander freely within the open-hearted space of Womanhood.

So maybe try something softer. Let's befriend our soft side and bring her out into the light. She needs more tender loving care than we can imagine. Give yourself the freedom to descend into your body, embrace your softer side, your joy, sorrow, hormones, exhaustion, dreams and desires.

I learned how to sit in meditation when I became intrigued with eastern thought and Buddha's teachings. My early practices involved the physical practice of yoga-asana, followed by sitting in meditation, and then reading Buddhist text. This combination felt like a puzzle coming together.

Still, my early attempts at practice were incredibly frustrating. I would go strong, then get discouraged, give up. Time would go by and I would go back again. I was alone. No one else I knew was interested in these things. But that's the hook. We may feel very supported in a group, class or on retreat, but we have to learn how to integrate it, bring it to life on our own.

Buddhism and it's beautiful principles hold my precious heart. I have learned how to not separate myself from the world. For me that's been huge, and I have adopted the art of meditation fully into my life. I've happily become a meditator, as opposed to someone who is hopeful about it but never actually makes it happen.

Now I see for miles and miles when I meditate. There is expansion and growth and inner evolution. I sit and I see. I am a seer at times. It feels natural to me, but even after years of practice, I am growing and learning new things about meditation. New ways of being in meditation.

The harder challenge is living in a world and culture where so many other things take precedence.

There are so many resources for meditation. In fact, you can spend days acquiring resources, downloading new apps, reading books and never actually get around to meditating.

Keep it simple by starting with a few minutes a day. With yoga, I always say "a little a lot." By this I mean that it's a lot to do a little bit each day. The same is true for meditation. Give yourself a little and it will grow over time into a core piece of your Loving Kindness path.

Silence

Somewhere we know that without silence
words lose their meaning, that without listening
speaking no longer heals, that without distance
closeness cannot cure.
Henri Nouwen

In order to do our good work in the world we need to rest our minds and take a break from the noise. When we get quiet and listen, we hear beneath the surface. It's an act of Loving Kindness for ourselves and our fellow humans.

Getting quiet is the first and most basic step we take to begin knowing who we are. It's also the most resisted practice. I witness time and again in my work how challenging it is to help people understand the art of creating quiet time. It's just not a priority in our culture. There are a million distractions and getting quiet is not compelling enough for most. Until there is a health, financial, or relationship crisis, most will ignore this calling.

Many of us feel completely knackered by all of the opinions, judgments, negativity, fear mongering, righteousness, nay-saying, confusion of the media. The social channels have become a very stressed place to wander into. It's like a river overflowing and we've got to learn to just dip a toe in now and then.

The volume is too high, and no one is listening. In our tumultuous times, personal rage and expression has become the new norm. In fact, if you aren't taking action and showing your anger, some consider you to be part of the problem. This feels very unloving. It creates a level of anxiety that is like a constant hum.

Silence is the only way to quiet that hum. When we enter deep silence, we can return to the world grounded in our true self and ready to live from our intentions, rather than just reacting to everything that comes.

This beautiful way of living is a gift we receive from cultivating silence.

I like the metaphor of listening, because in order to listen, we have to be silent. We have to be quiet inside, and hear what the other person is saying. This allows us to pause and calm ourselves.

Consider the difference between listening and hearing. One is active. The other is passive. But it's easier to listen to silence than to look at space. You can listen to the silence even when there is noise, and rest there -- silence in sound. I've often used this metaphor, silence in sound, to convey the idea that the silence, the space of mind itself, is always there, even when there is sound.

Creativity

Creativity takes Courage
Henry Matisse

Do you allow yourself time and space to create? When there is space, creativity is natural. Every day you create without claiming it. The way you brew your coffee, place your flowers in the vase, or even dress yourself can show your creativity.

What are your creative dreams? Keep a creative journal. Write in stream-of-consciousness style about what sort of creative aspects your life is calling for. How does your vocation feel to you? Does it leave you tired, drained, used up? Or does it allow you to create magic? Bringing things into the light is illuminating.

Make lists and connect them to plans, dreams. Look inside yourself and ask what is missing in the creative realm. Or be present with what has already been created and cherish that. The point is to be present with your creative process: Where has it been and what does it desire to move toward? Stay open to what experience organically unfolds. Silence your inner critic.

Our relationship to our inner artist has to be nurtured. In order to carve out some space to create, you may have to let go of energy-sucking tasks or ways you spend time that don't enliven your life or your creative needs. Having a life in which we feel a creative process in flow gives us that feeling of "right livelihood" and a connection to something that makes the world a more beautiful place.

Creativity tends to burst in spurts and once the door is opened, the world is your oyster.

It may manifest itself in something as simple as creating a healthy meal or as complex as designing a house.

You might begin with a little self-praise. Begin creating a timeline of everything you've created in the past five years. Think big and small. Reflect and write about it. You may be delighted to learn that you've done so much! Many of us are visual learners and seeing a body of work in writing inspires more creativity. Then ask yourself, "What do I still want to create in my life and in my work?"

Then unfetter yourself, turn off your filters and allow yourself to go there. Dream as though nothing stood between you and your creative dreams. No restrictions. What is calling to you?

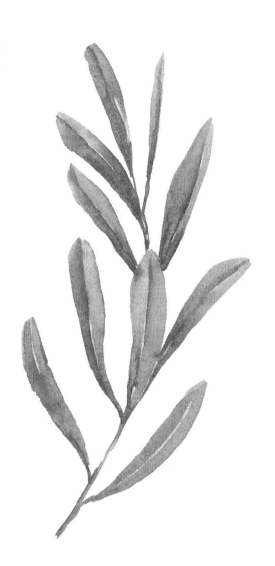

Listening

You know I have come to think listening is love,
that's what it really is.
Brenda Ueland

The beloved teachings on Loving Kindness guide us toward inner listening, solace and peace. Once we have listened to ourselves, we can give the gift of listening to others. For many, this is a gift they are longing for more than any physical thing. We are living in times where the simple act of listening has become both a lost art and a precious skill.

When I was a young woman I had the most amazing neighbor who became a very dear friend. Her greatest gift was that she would just listen to me without offering any opinion, judgment or negativity. She was an incredible listener, and teacher. I cherished her beautiful gift of presence in my life.

Listening in today's culture creates a holy silence. To generously open our hearts and give our complete attention to another is sweet relief in a world that never quiets. To place our attention on our intention. As a coach I cherish this part of my work the most.

Through the stories and sharing my clients entrust me with, I can see our sameness, our oneness. I'm constantly witnessing the truth in our human condition.

Listening has the power to heal, to connect and to to help us remember our dreams.

In many ways, listening is what we're doing as we meditate. We're pausing to pay attention to what's really happening in our body, mind and spirit.

Can you think of someone you know who is a great listener? Or someone who needs you to give the gift of listening. Listening can be easily practiced for a few moments every day as we interact with the people around us.

Writing

Write what should not be forgotten.

Isabel Allende

Keeping a journal is one of the most lovely practices of Loving Kindness. It helps me to integrate all of the other practices.

Writing can be a spiritual quest. It's a way we place ourselves in the moment and connect with our interior world. Like a prayer.

Moments of writing can feel completely timeless. The outside world can wait. It's a sacred act of being with oneself, and becoming completely absorbed by the space within the words.

The act of writing is very intentional and in the moment. In order to sit down and write I have to be able to pause other activities and focus. I pay attention in a way that I don't in other areas. Writing asks me to trust that whatever happens is ok. It's an uncertain process with great ambiguity. To not worry about the outcome but to be absorbed in the process.

Writing is a voice for my heart, soul and deepest yearnings. I consider writing a practice much like yoga, meditation, walking in the woods, traveling, cooking, even marriage.

Use the journal questions throughout this book to begin a daily writing practice if you do not already have one or need some inspiration. I find it helpful to write at the same time every day. I also carry my journal with me so I can write down a passing thought or a quote I read that I want to save.

There are lots of helpful books for getting started in writing. My favorite one is Anne Lamott's *Bird by Bird*. Lots of people have found their way into daily writing by following Julia Cameron's instructions for writing *Morning Pages*, a practice of writing whatever you are thinking every single morning.

Gratitude

Be thankful for what you have and you'll end up
having more. If you concentrate on what you don't have,
you'll never, ever have enough.

Oprah Winfrey

Gratitude is like self-love or self-care. We've been saturated lately with messages about the benefits of gratitude, and we agree that we need it. We believe we should be grateful. We wish everyone around us would be grateful. But are we actually practicing gratitude?

The simplest way I know to practice gratitude is to have a time every day where you say or write three things you are thankful for, not like a rote prayer of thanks for a meal, but rather, spending a minute surveying the day and choosing to give thanks for what you notice.

Another way you can practice gratitude even now is to take a moment to sit in stillness and consider the last several months of your life, or even the last year. Remember which people have made a difference in your life. Send them gratitude. Feel it flow from within you. When you show gratitude in this way, you are creating a wonderful energy in the world, a kind of healing vibration. Every year I practice cherishing where love grew and flourished in my life, thanking my students and retreaters for allowing me to be a part of their lives.

Buddhists believe that you cannot feel gratitude and be greedy at the same time. Gratitude is not about striving for achievements or money or reaching for more action and excitement, because gratitude resides in the present moment. In this moment, you can experience deep feelings of thankfulness and appreciation.

There are so many ways to practice gratitude. You can write a letter of thanks. You can send a text. You have no idea how your actions can add to the joy in the world, and when that happens, your own joy increases.

Retreats

And if travel is like love, it is, in the end,
mostly because it's a heightened state of awareness, in
which we are mindful, receptive, in dimmed by familiarity
and ready to be transformed. That is why the best trips,
like the best love affairs, never really end.
Pico Iyer

As a culture we are slipping further away from true rest and rejuvenation. Even as we are flooded with magazines and articles that emphasize wellness, people are still more stressed than ever.

Retreating has always been a beautiful way to celebrate the rhythms of life. It's an ancient practice.

But we have forgotten it. Our culture is all about speed, efficiency, and shortcuts, so it is almost impossible to allow for the retreat, rest or reflection our bodies, minds and spirits crave.

Some days we experience glimpses of goodness or small moments of peace, but those are just scratching the surface.

The relevance and need for deep, soothing rest for our souls is at an all time high, but the practice of it, is at an all time low.

This seems strange when we consider how many wellness choices, retreat centers, workshops, and events are available to us. We have more options than ever before for retreating, but it's still terribly difficult for people to make the break. Even people with plenty of money will find a reason why they can't unwind, enjoy life more, let it go.

There is almost no margin of our lives in which work, media and frenzy does not take up space, and this seems normal to us. We are becoming so geared toward overfunctioning, and we praise each other for being busy. We lack the ability to make choices where our health, our joy, our fun and our lightness of being do not take a back seat.

Sometimes I think that we are on the verge of a huge paradigm shift when it comes to retreating. We have all the proof we need that our current way of living is not making us happy, but right now the conversation is at a low murmur. We aren't succeeding at raising our vibration as a culture and feeling healthier and happier even though we are surrounded by images of yoga mats and self care hashtags.

In fact, sometimes the pictures make it worse. We see images of a yoga teacher with a serene face on Instagram and we can't figure out why we can't paint that image on to our own lives. But true yoga is not about a perfectly framed photo or designer workout clothing. In fact, that's the very opposite of yoga. The word *yoga* has its roots in the word *unity*. Becoming connected to ourselves and aligning our body, mind and spirit is the practice of yoga. And it takes all the time and energy we can give to it, because it is a lifetime practice.

Yoga and meditation are not necessarily a blissed-out place. In my experience it can be very messy, very entangled emotionally. And a yoga teacher is not meant to be a guru. The teacher has their own struggles and days of holy terror, but they can teach others how to take the next step on the path to wellness. The commercial images of yoga can taint our practice by causing us to set up unkind expectations for ourselves. Even worse, we can surround ourselves with wellness images and shop for the perfect yoga mat or essential oils, but never get around to the actual practice of yoga.

Even though we have more hype, media and energy around the dream of wellness, we have no idea how to embrace and integrate it into daily life on a regular basis.

If we do not ever retreat or truly rest, we raise the stakes on our health risks. High blood pressure, adrenals on fire, stress hormones on the rise, problems with sleep, digestion and intimacy are on the light list.

Overall when we look at our life from a holistic point of view, it's not hard to see where the misalignment is. We practice bits and pieces like healthy foods now and then, a squeezed-in meditation, a workout here, a yoga class there, or a quick weekend getaway. Yet we never really go deep.

So we are missing out on an immersion into true rejuvenation.

The antidote to our addicted-to-speed way of life is that we have to create the conditions for retreating, outside the norm of daily life. We have to take a stand, make a commitment and get devoted to retreating before we become ill, burned out, exhausted or depressed.

We need space and places to untether, to align, to come back, to dream again, to practice all forms of self-care and love, to be with ourselves.

On a retreat we have time to really know ourselves and return to self-belief. To hush. To enter many of the other Loving Kindness practices.

A retreat is like a deep dive into Loving Kindness. It can jumpstart a new practice or deepen and extend an old one. I believe there is magnanimous power in going away for extended periods, and really sinking into a full experience body, mind and spirit.

A retreat is different from a vacation in that it is more than rest or sight-seeing. A retreat has to have space to restore what we have lost, to find healing or to join in a joyful dance with Loving Kindness.

There is no question that retreats are important investments in well-being and reflection, not frivolous indulgences. I've devoted over twenty years of my life to educating people on this subject. It has not been an easy road, and my experience is now coming full circle as I go deeper into my third decade as a retreat leader, teacher and coach.

In my work with taking people on retreat, I've witnessed how it takes days for people to truly come down off their high stress life. It's quite difficult to let go of control and just be. A weekend retreat barely scratches the surface. You need at least a week for true retreat.

When I recommend retreats to my students, they often have a really hard time justifying taking such good care of themselves.

Sometimes when they do go on retreat, they spend huge chunks
of time feeling guilty and anxious. We are so used to putting
something or someone else first. As the world becomes increasingly
more violent, we tend to micro control what is closest to us. Then it
becomes impossible to take a break for healing and rest.

If we aren't careful, we could lose the qualities retreat nurtures in
ourselves, and in our culture. I'm grateful to work deeply with people
on retreat, because I get to watch them learn ways of being that they
can take home. When we have learned the art of retreat within our
daily lives, we shift into living a life that remains awake to Loving
Kindness.

Slowness

Be happy in the moment, that's enough.
Each moment is all we need, not more.
Mother Teresa

In the west, we're just beginning to envision how practice is a way of being. We want to already be there. We have to learn how to slow down, be patient and really kind to ourselves. As a pioneering society with productivity and accomplishment at the core of who we are, there is a certain struggle. If we can learn to accept the quality of these practices as clear and direct it's a great start. We start right where we are. Each moment lets us begin again and again.

Remember Mama Italy. She is calling you to slow down.

This list of practices is certainly not exhaustive. There are so many ways to practice Loving Kindness. To notice, to feel, to see, to appreciate. To take the time to be fully present with what is happening in the moments of your days. To live simply and unfetter your days, ambitions and preferences. To move your body. To know when you need rest, to pause, to reach out to a friend or loved one. To listen, to be right where you are. As your practice grows, so will the ways you practice.

When you read through all of these practices, inevitably your mind can begin to churn out thoughts of ways you must "do more." You might think, "I'm going to start meditating for an hour every morning" or "I'm going to be silent this Saturday." Our brains are so trained to keep lists and to turn our lives into calendars. Of course, I encourage you to add these practices to your life in whatever ways are possible. But for now, soften the part of yourself that wants to make you "do more." Use this closing meditation to return again to this present moment.

A Softening Meditation:

Sit down on the ground or a comfortable chair.

Settle in, feel your body settling down.

Take a slow deep breath in, long slow exhale and let your shoulders drop.

Feel into your body. Notice where you're holding tension.

Gently say "Now it's time for me to pause into this moment. It's time for me to give myself these moments to stop pushing and trying to fix something."

Gently say "I can be here right now and be ok with whatever is happening within me or around me."

Continue sitting and letting your body untense. Notice how your exhale helps you feel softer and more tender within.

Make a wish for yourself to remember that sitting quietly and practicing like this might not always be comfortable. It's ok to sit and be curious about what it feels like.

Nothing needs to be solved.

Breathing in peace, breathing out calm. I'm here. I am.

Journaling Questions

What is one simple way you can remain close to Loving Kindness practice today?

Journaling Questions

My Loving Kindness Blessing

Dear heart,

Daily life often takes enormous amounts of energy.

*If I could wish one thing for you it would be
that you cut yourself some serious Loving Kindness slack.*

Life is fleeting, we need to practice savoring it more than we do.

But it is just that, a practice. Life, love and meaning.

In everything, just practice.

*Sometimes our ego steps in and tries to take over.
The ego is not a bad thing. We need it to do important things in life.
It's just that we need to tame that ego beast.
We need to let the ego know when the soul needs rest.*

You can lighten up and still have a full life I promise.

In fact when you practice getting off your own back on a regular basis, you'll discover the joy in it and want to do it more.

You will have time to smell the flowers.

You will be able to look into the eyes of a loved one and let it be all there is.

Loving Kindness is what carries us like a boat gently sailing across the sea. Through it we're able to glimpse how we can turn wisdom into joy.

It's so much deeper than we imagine. Growing Loving Kindness increases well-being, happiness, energy and empathy. It transforms the mundane to the magical. It is your heart of gold.

May it be so for you, dear heart.

May you know Loving Kindness each day for yourself.

May you grow into sharing it with others.

May you be happy.

May you be at peace.

XO,
Jane

Appendix I:

SACRED PRACTICES
FOR THE SEASONS

As our ancestors have done from the beginning of time, we honor the cycles and the seasons that remind us of the ever-changing flow of life of which we are a part.

Ritual acts give life meaning. They also honor and acknowledge the unseen web of life that connects us all. I've been adding more rituals to my life in the past few years and feel a huge shift of inner knowing and peace because of it.

If you don't have a sangha (community) or place to practice ritual, don't be afraid to create your own and reclaim your connection to the source of all life. You can also bless others by inviting them into your rituals and ceremonies.

A simple act done with intention in your heart is enough. Always keep Loving Kindness in mind during your practice.

There is great healing energy found in nature.

The new moon says: rest, meditate, eat healthy, drink water and teas, and practice appreciating what you have. The new moon is an ideal time to plant seeds of growth, shift and loving kindness. The full moon is a time of high energy and power, a perfect time for releasing what no longer serves you in order to make space for something new. A waning moon can also be the perfect time to let things go.

The solstices and equinoxes mark the changing of the seasons and the changes in our lives.

They are a great time for sitting down to write, to mark a few intentions.

What is it that you want to bring into your life?

You may literally want to write it on a piece of paper and plant what you wrote into the ground somewhere in your yard or home.

Light a candle and make a sacred moment for those wishes.

Rituals help to bring our practices to life, and bring more joy to our life as well.

Here are some ideas for creating rituals and ceremonies to bring Loving Kindness into your life in every season.

Spring Equinox Ceremony

Come with me into the woods. Where spring is advancing,
as it does, no matter what, not being singular or particular,
but one of the forever gifts, and certainly visible.

Mary Oliver

March is the month of all things unfurling, seeding, expanding and...

All things Magnanimous.

Doesn't that word just evoke a sense of big-hearted love?

Spring is a good time to feel *the greatness of your own spirit.* It's a claim I have attempted to make for myself and I have worked to pass that wisdom along to my clients.

The virtue of being great of mind and heart is a soothing balm for what ails us.

In Buddhist thought, the quality of being magnanimous stems from the loftiness of spirit enabling one to bear trouble calmly, to disdain meanness and pettiness, and to display a noble generosity.

Questions for reflection during the spring equinox could be:

How can we grow more Loving Kindness into our heart?

What practices help us embody more loving feelings, each day?

Tell me, has there ever been a time in humanity where those qualities wouldn't serve us? Has there ever been a time where those qualities wouldn't help us to let compassion rule our emotions and strengthen our hope for the human condition?

I highly recommend spending time journaling on this topic during the month of March. Follow the breadcrumbs and see what magic you will encounter. Remember that journaling may be viewed as a spiritual practice, one of great self-care for the heart.

When you externalize your feelings, dreams, yearnings, sorrows and joys, you shift the way you process and think about them. It's a cathartic and healing practice where your voice is allowed to take flight.

As we approach the Spring Equinox, the body, mind and spirit may become restless and anxious. We're shedding winter and entering a new season so it's natural to feel a deep shift within. Move through seasonal changes through the art of being more tender and gentle with our days.

We need space and places to untether, to align, to come back, to dream again, to practice all forms of self-care and love, to be with ourselves. To really know ourselves and return to self-belief. To hush.

On the Spring Equinox, write down on a small piece of paper what practices you want to grow more of, ways you can bring more Loving Kindness to life. Bury the list in the ground, along with a new plant or some seeds, so that you can literally watch it grow this spring.

Have a loving March and keep peace in your heart.

Summer Solstice Ceremony

The Summer Solstice is not a time for modesty.
The wild world is not shy about its beauty and gifts.
Plants and creatures are engaged in a no-holds-barred
life-fest of blossoming and flourishing,
each according to its unique essence, place, and purpose
in this glorious weaving of Mother Earth.
The Path of She, by Karen Clark

Summer is the time of fruition in the natural world, and our internal world feels it on the most vibrant and subtle level.

There is no better invitation than the bloom of summer to rise up, step into and embrace our strengths, our desires, our callings and to own our belonging on this earth.

As many of my long time yoga students have heard me say, "you can't harden into" advanced yoga poses. The way in is through some combination of softening yet focused effort, relaxing the mind grip and freeing up our inherent ability to own all of who we are in this moment, and who we are becoming.

We may never feel that we've arrived and that's the beauty of it.

Note the lioness.

She is awake. She stands proud and alert. She may appear at ease in the moment and yet her power is unleashed not by hardening or pushing, but by actually rising into it and letting go of the shackles. Without the grip, the power is strong and precise.

The lioness reminds us that we need to stay in our power and focus.

We've got to sit down in our life and be with it.

One thing I hear time and time again from my coaching clients is how challenging it is for them to sit down and be quiet. To not be distracted by their phone, shopping, food, talking, anything other than just Being.

For the week before and after the summer solstice, practice "being." Cultivate a ritual to enhance spiritual focus, inner wisdom and brave heart.

Start simple, be repetitive and follow the breadcrumbs.

Go outside in nature and thank Mother Earth, Sun, and Moon for their blessings and offerings so generously offered to us each and every day.

Thankfulness always creates internal harmony in our central nervous system, helping us to feel less anxiety and more internal peace.

For your simple summer solstice ceremony, sit down somewhere outside and breathe in deeply, exhale slowly and repeat over and over, let the mind settle, stare at the sky, a body of water or the stars.

Give yourself the freedom to take a break from the world.

Allow yourself to be emboldened enough to rise into what is coming next, even if you don't have it all sorted out.

Be intentional and open to receiving what is yours to claim.

Claim your gifts and blessings.

Know that rising into your strengths doesn't involve grasping or gripping. Always remember Loving Kindness. It is an act of letting the body, mind and spirit receive as oppose to taking.

It's your time to flourish and blossom.

Autumn Equinox Ceremony

Autumn is a second spring when every leaf is a flower.
Albert Camus

If spring and summer are a time for allowing new things to grow, sometimes autumn can be for reflection.

Autumn seems to have memory.

For an autumn equinox ceremony, you have full permission to declare your complete range of emotions and lessons, highs and lows, and everything in between.

All of it.

Joy, sorrow, fear, pain, bad attitude, envy, success, mean spirited actions, generosity, curiosity, melancholy, abundance, confusion, clarity, supported ideas, unsupported ideas, love, loss....ALL of it.

Sometime we need the most fierce reminder that adversity is where we really grow as a person, and that having things work out exactly the way we desire is great, but the stuff that keeps us awake at night is where we transform and transcend.

To be able to identify where our pain points are, to get real about it, is where we expand our consciousness and become more of who we are meant to be in this one precious life.

And in order to do that, we have to spend time figuring out who we really are.

What do I like? What do I think about that? What are my deepest desires? Who am I when no one is looking?

To know who we truly are, without the filter of a list of shoulds from a partner, sister, mother, friend or a society that is frankly a bit wonky - is such a magnanimous gift.

Sadly, for many people it's too painful to look, to bring our shadowy self into the light. We fear what it might mean. What changes it might bring.

So we stay stuck. We stay in the "unknowing."

It's not always that we consciously choose that either. It's just that sometimes it's too hard, or too exhausting to go there.

We need helpers to become knowers.

I've been there.

I've walked this path of light and shadow. I feel you.

A few years ago I was so tired of listening to some of my stories. Just so ready to move on.

I wanted to put away some of my burdens, to heal my past, to get on with my good work in the world.

I just felt so stuck...so down.

At that stage of life, I was no longer being served by going back.

I needed to propel forward.

But it took some time to reach this realization. I had to stop doing and spend time resting and reflecting, so that I could know my next steps instead of continuing to do the same things.

Here are a few questions for you to ponder as you enter the reflection and remembering of autumn. Use them as an autumn equinox meditation or journaling exercise.

What is the one thing you want to say but are afraid to?

What desires have emerged from your life this year?

How well do you know your true feelings? Can you speak of them?

How well do you really know yourself? Do you want to know more?

What is on your happiness calendar? How will you find more pleasure and joy?

You deserve to know those answers and knowing them is going to heal you and everyone around you.

This is how we heal the planet one person at a time.

Winter Solstice Ceremony

The simplicity of winter has a deep moral.
The return of nature, after such a career of splendor and
prodigality, to habits so simple and austere, is not lost
either upon the head or the heart. It is the philosopher
coming back from the banquet and the wine
to a cup of water and a crust of bread.
John Burroughs

On December 21, we move toward the return of the sun, the winter solstice time. This is one of my absolute favorite celebrations of the year. Winter solstice has been one of the most celebrated times of the year for as long as life has been recorded. The shift is so significant that I always set aside more time to mark and celebrate it in my own life, often with friends or family.

Yogasana is a meaningful ritual that keeps us connected to the ever changing flow of life through our breathing and body.

In yoga we can drop the story line and listen to what our body wants us to know. We can learn how to sit with our emotional landscape and not get carried into places that take us off center.

Our body always knows.

I like to practice slowing down when I'm preparing and eating at this time of year. Taking stock of how I'm nourishing my body for pleasure and sustenance. Feeling gratitude for food itself. Sensing the taste of food, feeling how my body responds to what I'm eating. Feeling feeling feeling!

We spend so much time shutting things out to stay calm. This time of year beckons us to pay careful attention in the most loving way. Give yourself this gift of presence.

Here are a few of my favorite winter solstice rituals to celebrate this pivotal moment in time as we venture inward to kindle our inner fire.

Feel free to adjust them or mix them up to create the ritual that feels right for you on December 21.

A Candlelit Day

Imagine what it would be like to spend the entire day without any artificial light? Consider welcoming in the darkness by lighting candles or lanterns instead of turning on the lights on the solstice. Bring light into this day by placing floating candles in bowls or vessels all around your home. Be creative as you surround yourself with little altars.

A Candlelight Ceremony

Invite your family or friends to join in this lovely ritual.

Place a large candle in the middle of a table with various smaller candles around it. Leave all the candles unlit.

Turn off all the lights and spend a moment in darkness, remembering and honoring the sun's light.

Then light the big candle in the middle and offer a blessing. Invite everyone else to come and light a smaller candle from the larger candle's flame and place it back on the table, smaller candles around the larger candle.

Once all candles are lit, a chant, song, blessing or "Happy Solstice" can be offered in unison.

This ceremony can also be enjoyed alone. As you light smaller candles from the large candle's flame, consider how the light within you spreads to others around you during this season.

Bell Ringing Ceremony

This ceremony is my favorite way to mark the solstice. It can take a simple form of the family ringing bells together at the moment of solstice, or it can be a longer circle ceremony similar to the candlelit ceremony. This ceremony is lovely even if just two people participate, but it is particularly fun for children so I will describe it as a family ceremony but of course you can adjust it for any group.

Gather together some bells of varying sizes and types that blend well with each other when rung together. Brass bells and/or jingle bells are commonly available and have long time associations with the season.

Each person present chooses a bell to ring. For a bell ringing solstice circle, everyone gathers together in a circle. Each has a bell in hand to ring. Parent(s) or some other family member serves as facilitator(s). She/he begins by saying a few words about the solstice being the start of the new solar year and that the calendar year is still structured today in many places around the world on the solar year.

The facilitator then describes how bells have been rung in connection with many types of celebrations. Bells have been rung at this time of year to ring out the old year and to ring in the new year. Then the facilitator invites the family to celebrate the solstice with bells.

If you wish to honor the directions as part of a spiritual practice (Native American, Buddhist, Christian, etc.), you can have the family divide up to face each of the compass points (North, East, South, West) and ring the bells in unison, honoring connections with each sacred direction. Then face one another for ringing the bells in the three directions connected with the center: upward, the place of the cosmos; downward, the place of the planet; and center; Divine unity.

In place of or in addition to individual direction honoring, the family rings all their bells together to celebrate their connection with each other as a family; then they ring them in unison again to celebrate their connection with the cycles of Nature; and then they ring them a third time in unison to celebrate their connection with life on planet Earth and all of Nature.

To close the ceremony, from the oldest to the youngest, each family member speaks a vision or wish for the planet for the coming year. After each one speaks, all ring bells together to affirm that vision/wish. After everyone has shared, the ceremony ends as the family calls out 'Happy Solstice' three times and rings bells.

Fire Ceremony

This can be done as a personal ceremony or with a group. Build a fire outside or use your indoor fireplace if you wish. Begin by giving out small pieces of paper and pencils and have each person write down something that they want to release.

When all have their papers ready, gather around the fire, and each person takes a turn to come to the fire and throw their paper in.

After everyone has a turn, seal the ritual by making loud noises all together. You can use drums, shakers or just your voices making a celebratory howl!

However you celebrate the solstice, whether pausing alone in quiet reflection or celebrating with loved ones, know that all over our planet, we are joining in Spirit as we do the same.

We honor our diversity to each other as humans and the planet as a larger holistic force.

Solstice Blessings to us all!

OM OM OM

Appendix II:

DIY LOVING KINDNESS RETREAT

As I mentioned in the section on retreats, getting away is such an important part of deepening your Loving Kindness practice. I would love for everyone to join me on a Loving Kindness retreat to Italy or on one of my retreats in Minnesota. But I want you to know that if joining an organized retreat is not accessible to you at this moment, you can still have the experience of a retreat by carving out time and space for yourself. Here are some guidelines, meditations and journaling questions for your own retreat. May they be helpful to you on your path to Loving Kindness.

What you seek is seeking you.
Rumi

Retreating is in many ways about your mindset. You can have a mini retreat every day for an hour if you get in the practice of carving out silence and sacred space around you. But if you find yourself unable to ignore the dishes or the laundry, or if you are distracted by the other people in your home, then I recommend setting aside at least a weekend to go away for a Loving Kindness Retreat.

Book yourself a room or small house an hour away from your home, somewhere close to nature. Make a large pot of soup or a big tupperware of salad that you can eat on all weekend, something nourishing and wholesome, but simple. Pack nuts and fruits and herbal teas. A journal and a pair of tennis shoes.

A few days before your Loving Kindness Retreat, spend some time setting yourself an intention: Here's what I want to give myself during this time away. Your intention will set the tone for your time. Come outside of yourself enough to plan the weekend like you are planning for someone you really love, who needs Loving Kindness.

That someone that you really love is YOU! Even if you don't feel it, you can manifest that Loving Kindness for yourself by giving yourself the gift of retreat. This retreat is not about doing something for yourself because you deserve it. If that's the case, you will easily cancel it or shorten it the moment you no longer think you "deserve" this time. Instead think of this Loving Kindness Retreat as **deep replenishment for your heart so you can fully show up to your life and work in the world.**

This replenishment is something we all need more of. Most of us are running on empty, living each day feeling like there is never enough time.

Taking a Loving Kindness Retreat counterintuitively takes away that concern of "never enough" by slowing time down.

So leave behind all work and "to do" lists. Turn off your phone. Enter deep time on your Loving Kindness Retreat.

Repeat your intention from your departure to your arrival, and it will guide your time. Only you will know if you need to book spa treatments or to pack your watercolors. Let your heart be your ultimate guide.

Here are my suggestions for some simple activities on your retreat. I would caution not to plan too much. Allow yourself time to sit with your own soul. Loving Kindness is patient, not busy, so give plenty of space.

Practice a Loving Kindness Meditation

Sit comfortably where you can be still for a while. Close your eyes and think of the kind of love a new mother has for her child. As pictures come to your mind, nurture in your heart the kind of deep, abiding love we think of as "motherly." Maybe it will be a mom and child you have been around, or maybe it will be the love you had for your babies. Spend a few minutes connecting to that love. Fill up a large pitcher with that love.

Now picture yourself sitting where you are now and imagine that pitcher of love being poured out over you. Bathe in Loving Kindness. Don't hurry. Just sit with the sensation of something being poured over you. Imagine it as love. Connect to loving yourself in this moment.

Next, you can begin to take that same pitcher of love and pour it over yourself in all the images of yourself that come to mind. Maybe earlier in the week you had a fight with your partner. Pause that memory and walk over to yourself and pour Loving Kindness out. Take a moment to accept that love, to connect with it, even in a moment you may not find yourself very lovable.

You can sit with this exercise for an hour or a whole day, remembering and pausing moments where you pour this pitcher of love out. Happy moments or sad moments or even neutral moments may come to mind. Maybe you see yourself standing at the sink washing dishes or carrying groceries into the house. You can meet yourself in even the mundane moments with this pitcher of love.

When you've spent as long as you want with this exercise, you can raise your hands in front of you. Picture that love being physically poured out one more time and fold it into your heart as you close your meditation.

Journal

I always find it helpful to spend time journaling on retreat, so if there are things that come up for you, images you want to remember, take the time to write them down.

Take a Nap

When you are tired, Loving Kindness tucks you into a real bed with blankets, rather than sitting up in a chair where you wake up with a creaky neck. Consider even using an eye mask. If you don't want to sleep for too long, you can set an alarm, but make the room dark and give yourself the gift of a true rest.

Journal:

What is the best sleep you can ever remember having?

Engage in the Japanese practice of shinrin-yoku

Shinrin-yoku translates as "forest bathing," or luxuriating in the woods. It is a truly mindful way of spending time in nature where you become especially focused on what you see, hear and smell. Your average walk in the park may help you relax a little, but *shinrin-yoku,* developed in Japan in the 1980s, is all about deliberately engaging with nature using all five senses. Portions of *shinrin-yoku* are done in silence. Cell phones are left behind.

"I encourage walkers to practice deep breathing and to tune in to what sparks their senses, like the texture of birch bark or the scent of wild flowers or pinecones," says Mark Ellison, who began teaching *shinrin-yoku* classes three years ago at Cabarrus College of Health Sciences in Concord, North Carolina. Take time to stop and touch the trees or the plants. Go slowly. Breathe deeply. There is nothing to hurry back for, so you can bathe for as long as you like in whatever green space is available to you.

Journal:

If you like, you can spend some time writing about your walking meditation.

On your *shinrin-yoku* walk, what did you notice that you might not have noticed in other walks?

Taste Your Food

Take the time to prepare even the simplest of meals on a plate. Slice your fruit or set up your salad like you are serving it to someone else. You are the special guest of your retreat! So set your table. Make it beautiful. Give thanks. Go slowly, chewing each bite or holding each mouthful a bit longer to sense the smells and tastes.

Journal:

What foods nourish you most? What food makes you feel good? What do you notice about your meals when you eat slowly and in silence?

Use this book!

This short book on Loving Kindness is full of meditations and journal exercises that you can repeat throughout your life to shed light on your path towards Loving Kindness. It is my hope that through this book, you will find that your own path unfolds itself more and more to you and that you will learn that with each new day, you have an opportunity to bring more Loving Kindness to your life and to the world.

I wish you peace and happiness as you journey with Loving Kindness!

Acknowledgements

To all the Bodhisattvas. May they illuminate the truth for all of eternity.

To my husband Jesse and his authentic solid love, support, life vision.

To my children Brandon and Ivy, my grandchildren Audrey and Dean, June, my nieces, nephews, extended family and neighbors all over the world for their love.

To my Grandmother Elvira for her gentle quiet heart.

To my Mother and Father for giving me life, opening my eyes and shaping my vision.

To the woods, the trees and natural world for their never ending enchantments.

To Steve Haney for showing me the ways of the Q'ero.

To Tenzin Palmo for opening the door in 2000.

To all of my yoga students, retreaters, coaching clients, dear friends, who have taught me the most about how to be more of who I naturally am.

To all of my teachers past, present, future.

To Lianne Raymond for her unique perspective, healing words and loving support.

To Alison Chino for her soft heart, keen eye, and deep wisdom. And for helping me with everything that has to do with writing this book.

To my eternal zest for life.

Made in the USA
Middletown, DE
04 October 2018